Cross-Cultural Encounters

Studies in Chinese Christianity

G. Wright Doyle and Carol Lee Hamrin,
Series Editors
A Project of the Global China Center
www.globalchinacenter.org

Previously published volumes in the series

Carol Lee Hamrin & Stacey Bieler, eds., *Salt and Light: Lives of Faith That Shaped Modern China*, volume 1

Carol Lee Hamrin & Stacey Bieler, eds., *Salt and Light: More Lives of Faith That Shaped Modern China*, volume 2

Richard R. Cook & David W. Pao, eds., *After Imperialism: Christian Identity in China and the Global Evangelical Movement*

Carol Lee Hamrin & Stacey Bieler, *Salt and Light: More Lives of Faith That Shaped Modern China*, volume 3

Lit-sen Chang, *Wise Man from the East: Lit-sen Chang (Zhang Lisheng)*

George Hunter McNeur, *Liang A-Fa: China's First Preacher, 1789–1855*

Eunice V. Johnson, *Timothy Richard's Vision: Education and Reform in China, 1880–1910*

G. Wright Doyle, *Builders of the Chinese Church: Pioneer Protestant Missionaries and Chinese Church Leaders*

Jack R. Lundbom, *On the Road to Siangyang: Covenant Mission in Mainland China 1890–1949*

Brent Fulton, *China's Urban Christians: A Light That Cannot Be Hidden*

Andrew T. Kaiser, *The Rushing on of the Purposes of God: Christian Missions in Shanxi since 1876*

Li Ma & Jin Li, *Surviving the State, Remaking the Church: A Sociological Portrait of Christians in Mainland China*

Linda Banks and Robert Banks, *Through the Valley of the Shadow: Australian Women in War-Torn China*

Arthur Lin, *The History of Christian Missions in Guangxi, China*

Linda Banks and Robert Banks, *They Shall See His Face: The Story of Amy Oxley Wilkinson and Her Visionary Work among the Blind in China*

Wayne Ten Harmsel, *The Registered Church in China: Flourishing in a Challenging Environment*

Cross-Cultural Encounters

China and the Reformed Church in America

Edited by
GLORIA SHUHUI TSENG

Foreword by
DENNIS N. VOSKUIL

◆PICKWICK *Publications* • Eugene, Oregon

CROSS-CULTURAL ENCOUNTERS
China and the Reformed Church in America

Studies in Chinese Christianity

Copyright © 2021 Wipf and Stock Publishers. All rights reserved. Except for brief quotations in critical publications or reviews, no part of this book may be reproduced in any manner without prior written permission from the publisher. Write: Permissions, Wipf and Stock Publishers, 199 W. 8th Ave., Suite 3, Eugene, OR 97401.

Pickwick Publications
An Imprint of Wipf and Stock Publishers
199 W. 8th Ave., Suite 3
Eugene, OR 97401

www.wipfandstock.com

PAPERBACK ISBN: 978-1-5326-1891-8
HARDCOVER ISBN: 978-1-4982-4480-0
EBOOK ISBN: 978-1-4982-4479-4

Cataloging-in-Publication data:

Names: Tseng, Gloria Shuhui, editor. | Voskull, Dennis N., foreword.

Title: Cross-cultural encounters : China and the Reformed Church in America / edited by Gloria Shuhui Tseng ; foreword by Dennis N. Voskull.

Description: Eugene, OR: Pickwick Publications, 2021. | Studies in Chinese Christianity. | Includes bibliographical references and index.

Identifiers: ISBN: 978-1-5326-1891-8 (paperback). | ISBN: 978-1-4982-4480-0 (hardcover). | ISBN: 978-1-4982-4479-4 (ebook).

Subjects: LCSH: Christianity—China—History—19th century. | Christianity—China—History—20th century. | Reformed Church in America—Missions—China. | Otte, J. A.

Classification: BV3415.2 C85 2021 (print). | BV3415.2 (ebook).

Contents

Foreword by Dennis Voskuil | vii
Acknowledgments | ix
List of Photos |
Introduction by Gloria S. Tseng | xi

1. A Visionary Mission: The Life and Work of Dr. J. A. Otte | 1
   —Rebekah Llorens

2. Cultural Exchange: The Story of William Angus and His Poetry | 22
   —Eric Dawson

3. The Dual Calling of Missionary Wives: Married Women Missionaries of the RCA in China, 1917–1951 | 42
   —Victoria Longfield

4. Hope and Wilhelmina Hospital School of Nursing: The Role of Missionary Nurses in Xiamen, China | 58
   —Katelyn Dickerson

5. Tena Holkeboer: Single and Female in the China Mission of the Reformed Church in America, 1920–1948 | 78
   —Gloria S. Tseng and Madalyn DeJonge

6. Faith and Humanitarian Aid in Wartime China, 1937–1941 | 106
   —Claire Barrett

Foreword

Dennis Voskuil

THE REFORMED CHURCH IN America began its work in China in 1842 when the Reverend David Abeel arrived in the port city of Amoy (now Xiamen) located on an island off the southeast coast of the mainland. Long determined to establish a Christian mission in China, Abeel sailed to Amoy at an opportune time near the end of the Opium War (1839-42) during which Chinese military forces were easily defeated by the British. China was forced to sign the Treaty of Nanking (1842), which stipulated that the Chinese must open five port cities, including Amoy, for trade with Western nations. The Treaty of Nanking was a prime example of gun-boat diplomacy and Western imperialism. The Amoy mission took root under the protection of a colonial power.

One of the persistent criticisms of Western missionary efforts during the nineteenth century has been the charge that the introduction of the Christian faith was itself an example of cultural and religious imperialism. In essence, this critique of the Christian missions is centered in the conviction that dominant Western values and beliefs were imposed upon non-Western cultures. In their studies of various aspects of the Amoy mission of the RCA, each of the authors of this volume underscores the cultural interactions between the Chinese and the RCA missionaries. It is evident that cultural influences always moved in two directions. The Chinese certainly embraced many of the ideals and practices introduced by those from the West, but it was just as true that the missionaries were also absorbing and embracing the ideals and practices of the Chinese. This does not mean that forms of colonialism and Western imperialism cannot be identified, but that cultural interchange is much more complex than often described.

When the People's Republic of China established itself during the early 1950s, the members of the Amoy Mission either returned to the United States or were relocated to work in Chinese communities outside mainland China, mainly in Taiwan and the Philippines. Some observers were convinced that the Christian faith, scorned and suppressed by the Communist regime, would essentially die away in China. Of course, that did not happen, and now China has a fast-growing Christian population.

A number of years ago when I was president of Western Theological Seminary, an RCA institution which trained many of the hundred or more missionaries who served the Amoy Mission over the years, Christian visitors from the region of Amoy arrived one day unannounced. Accompanied by Chinese government officials, this group of visitors spoke to our community during our morning coffee time. They indicated that they came to the seminary because they wished to express appreciation to the RCA and the seminary for sending those who were devoted to introducing the Gospel in the region of Amoy. It was a memorable moment.

The editor of this volume is Professor Gloria Tseng, a member of the Department of History at Hope College in Holland, Michigan. The essays that are included here were written by her students who participated in summer research projects on the Amoy Mission from 2013 to 2014. The primary research materials were available through the Joint Archives of Holland located in the Theil Research Center on the campus of Hope College. Because many of the Reformed Church missionaries who served in China were graduates of Hope College and Western Theological Seminary, their papers were entrusted to the Joint Archives of these institutions, making them accessible to the student researchers.

Professor Tseng was assisted in the project by Marc Baer, a former chair of the Department of History, who cobbled together some financial support for student research through the Pagenkopf History Research Scholarship. In addition, she received two Nyenhuis Faculty-Student Collaborative Research Grants. She is also grateful to Wright Doyle of the Global China Center for expressing interest in having this volume appear in the Studies in Chinese Christianity series that he co-edits with Carol Hamrin for Wipf and Stock.

Acknowledgments

THIS VOLUME CAME AS a result of two summers of faculty-student collaborative research in 2013 and 2014. Special thanks go to Geoffrey Reynolds, the archivist, for guiding our students through the rich collection of missionary papers held at the Joint Archives of Holland, and for innumerable subsequent acts of assistance and service as I edited the volume. Heartfelt gratitude also goes to Marc Baer and the late Jonathan Hagood for our collaboration in mentoring our student researchers. One could not ask for more selfless and collegial colleagues. It was a deeply rewarding experience to share in the discoveries of the contributors of the essays in this volume. The men and women whose lives are presented in these essays served a God whose ways are above our ways, and whose thoughts are above our thoughts. May this work be an acceptable offering.

List of Photographs

The New Map of China Prepared for Missionaries
    and Travellers (1937) | 124

A map of the Amoy Mission, published by the RCA | 125

The cover of a Minnan (south Fujian) hymnal,
    Minnan Jidujiao Shengshi | 126

Hymn #50, "What a Friend We Have in Jesus,"
    from Minnan Jidujiao Shengshi | 127

Hope and Wilhelmina Hospital | 128

Restored Hope and Wilhelmina Hospital (2018) | 129

Students and staff of Hope and Wilhelmina Hospital (1936) | 130

Students of Hope and Wilhelmina Hospital (1940) | 131

Students and staff of Hope and Wilhelmina Hospital (1950) | 132

Class presidents and vice-presidents of the Girls' Middle School | 133

Delegates of the South Fujian United Synod to the Fourth General
    Assembly of the Church of Christ in China (1937) | 134

William and Joyce Angus celebrating Easter
    with a Chinese congregation | 135

Christina Wang and Tena Holkeboer | 136

Jean Nienhuis and Gim-siu Sio | 137

Introduction

Gloria S. Tseng

THE FIRST REFORMED CHURCH in America (RCA) missionary arrived in Xiamen, Fujian province, in 1842, immediately after the cessation of the hostilities of the First Opium War (1839–1842). The last group of RCA missionaries left China in 1951, shortly after the outbreak of the Korean War (1950–1953). At its height, in 1923, the RCA mission in Fujian had fifty-one missionaries in the field, twenty men and thirty-one women.[1] In this history of a little over one hundred years, war and unrest were a permanent reality, and China underwent significant transformation: the collapse of the last imperial dynasty (1911), the period of political fragmentation of the late 1910s and early 1920s, the short-lived Nationalist regime headed by Chiang Kai-shek (1928–1949), eight years of brutal war with and occupation by Japan (1937–1945), and finally civil war (1946–1949), which only came to an end with the founding of the People's Republic of China (1949). During this time, not only did political institutions change, but profound cultural and social changes also took place. Industrialization made its way into China's treaty ports. In the cities, gender and family norms evolved as Confucian values came under attack from the 1910s on by some of China's leading intellectuals, and by the 1930s even women's fashion had changed beyond recognition. Through all this, the RCA mission was both a historical witness and a historical actor.

---

1. De Jong, *The Reformed Church in China*, 339.

Introduction

A total of 151 RCA missionaries served with the denomination's Amoy[2] Mission during these hundred some years. Their lengths of service ranged from under a year to fifty-three years.[3] This was the era of career missionaries, many of whom spent an entire lifetime in the mission field. From its initial mission in Xiamen, the denomination expanded to the towns of Zhangzhou, Xiaoxi, Tong'an, and Longyan and their surrounding countryside.[4] In short, the RCA's Amoy Mission was relatively small; yet, its presence in Fujian province was deeply rooted and significant. The missionaries featured in this collection—John Otte (years of service 1887–1910), William Angus (1925–1951), Joyce Angus (1925–1951), Jeannette Veldman (1930–1951), Jean Nienhuis (1920–1951), Clarence Holleman (1919–1950), Ruth Holleman (1919–1950), Stella Veenschoten (1917–1951), Tena Holkeboer (1920–1948), Henry Poppen (1918–1951), William Vander Meer (1920–23 & 1926–1951), Alma Vander Meer (1923–1951)—covered a span from the last quarter of the nineteenth century to 1951, with only a nine-year gap from 1910 to 1919. Evangelists, pastors, teachers, nurses, and doctors numbered among them. Those who served in China during the Sino-Japanese War also became humanitarian aid workers. These missionaries were both observers and agents of change in China's tumultuous modern history. Seven of them were graduates of Hope College,[5] with whom the contributors of this volume share a special connection as fellow alumni.

The issues raised and topics covered in this volume—medical missions, gender and family, education, racial relations, cultural exchanges, modernity, and humanitarian aid—are all subjects of interest to the scholar or student of the history of Christian mission and the history of world Christianity. The History of Western Medicine in China Project co-sponsored by

2. The romanization for Xiamen used by the missionaries themselves.

3. This information is culled from the Appendix of De Jong, *The Reformed Church in China*, 347–49.

4. The romanizations used by RCA missionaries at the time for these locations were Changchow or Chiang-chiu, Sio-khe, Tong-an, and Leng-na, respectively. The missionaries used the local dialect in their form of romanization, whereas I have chosen to convert all place names in this volume to modern pinyin (based on Mandarin) for the sake of conformity with current romanization practices for Chinese in both the media and the scholarship on China. A few exceptions are personal and place names whose old romanizations are so well-known that they continue to be used frequently.

5. Special thanks go to Geoffrey Reynolds, who compiled this information. The graduates were John Otte, Henry Poppen, Ruth Holleman, William Vander Meer, Joyce Angus, Jeannette Veldman, and Tena Holkeboer.

INTRODUCTION

Indiana University-Purdue University Indianapolis and the Peking University Health Science Center produced an online resources portal in 2012.[6] The numerous digitized sources made available by the project bear witness to the essential role played by Christian medical missionaries in the development of Western medicine in modern China, a historical development that missionary doctor John Otte and missionary nurses Jeannette Veldman and Jean Nienhuis most likely did not foresee. At the time Otte was establishing hospitals in China, Holland, the city of Otte's alma mater, had no hospital.[7] The element of sacrificial giving in the missionary movement, despite its many shortcomings, is easily seen in this little fact.

Seven of the twelve missionaries featured in this volume were women. Even in this small sample, one must acknowledge the importance of women in the missionary enterprise. Female missionaries are the focus of two essays in this volume: Tena Holkeboer exemplified the accomplishments of and personal sacrifices made by single women in the mission field; Stella Veenschoten, Joyce Angus, and Ruth Holleman were three missionary wives who each contributed indispensably to "their husbands' ministries." Emily Manktelow's recent work on early nineteenth-century missionary families of the London Missionary Society in the Pacific and southern Africa is an example of the pertinence of gender and family as angles of analysis.[8]

Except John Otte, all the missionaries in this volume experienced the Sino-Japanese War and its attendant hardships. In the vast human misery caused by this undeclared war, which is best remembered for the infamous Rape of Nanking,[9] Christian missionaries exhibited great compassion and courage by offering relief to as many as they could in the midst of wartime shortages.[10] A number of RCA missionaries in Xiamen did likewise, setting up refugee camps in the International Settlement on

6. Indiana University-Purdue University Indianapolis, "The History of Western Medicine in China Resources Portal," http://ulib.iupui.edu/wmicproject/project (accessed October 6, 2017).

7. Holland Hospital, the city's first hospital was established in 1917, seven years after Otte's premature death. See Holland Hospital, "100 A New Century of Caring," http://100.hollandhospital.org/ (accessed October 6, 2017).

8. Manktelow, *Missionary Families*.

9. Nanjing in modern pinyin.

10. The Nanking Massacre Project (2008) of the Yale University Divinity School Library (https://web.library.yale.edu/divinity/digital-collections/nanking-massacre), Iris Chang's *Rape of Nanking* (1997), and Suping Lu's *They Were in Nanjing* (2004) document the essential role taken by missionaries in creating the Nanking International Safety Zone to shelter Chinese refugees from the wanton violence of Japanese soldiers.

the small island of Gulangyu[11] in response to the Japanese invasion of China's eastern provinces, and one of the essays in this collection explores wartime humanitarian aid as an aspect of the RCA's mission work. Meeting physical human needs has been part of the Gospel message since the days of Jesus and the disciples. In the post-World War Two and postcolonial era, Christians have done this through nongovernment and non-profit organizations. In the period with which this volume is concerned, China missionaries were on the forefront of famine and disaster relief, in addition to providing medical care, even before the Sino-Japanese War necessitated wartime relief. A cursory look into the flagship journal of Christian mission, *Missiology*, will make evident the continuing importance of this aspect of Christian mission: "Networking, Civil Society, and the NGO" by Stanley H. Skreslet (1997) and "Proclaiming the Reign of God in a Suffering World" by Kim Lamberty (2017).

Finally, but not least importantly, cross-cultural friendships developed between Western missionaries and Chinese Christians. One sees glimpses of these relationships—despite the reality of racial inequality and cultural barriers—in Angus's poems, in the mentoring of young Chinese nurses by Nienhuis and Veldman, and elsewhere. Friendship is a reciprocal relationship between equals, all the more remarkable in the larger context of nineteenth- and early twentieth-century Western imperialism, and of the increasingly strident anti-imperialist political rhetoric accompanying the rise of the Chinese Communist movement. The former did not negate the latter but stood as a witness against it, as a powerful expression of Christian love in an unjust world. Missionaries were products of their time. On the one hand, we see in Angus's poems the author's painful awareness of the nefarious effects of Western privilege on the Gospel witness of the church in China and his efforts to counter them. On the other hand, we see a glaring example of such privilege in Mrs. Veenschoten's complaints to family members in the US that she would rather have a modern stove and a vacuum cleaner than Chinese servants in her household in China. Such inequalities were the remarkable context in which early cross-cultural relationships developed.

As historian of world Christianity and Christian mission Dana Roberts argues movingly, friendships between missionaries and indigenous Christians mitigated the impact of colonialism and sowed the seed for the remarkable growth of world Christianity that we have witnessed in the

---

11. Referred to as Kulangsu by RCA missionaries.

Introduction

postcolonial era: "For unknown numbers of missionaries and indigenous Christian leaders in the early to mid-twentieth century, friendship was a potent yet underrecognized ethic and practice in the creation of world Christianity as a multicultural community. Indeed, without friendship as clear witness of Christlike love, the inequities and racism of the colonial era might have prevented the spread of Christianity across cultures."[12] One might add, for the sake of emphasis, that the way to "world Christianity as a multicultural community" was paved by Christlike love *as expressed in friendship, more so than in humanitarian aid*, even as desperately needed and altruistic as the latter was.

As Nicolas Standaert demonstrates effectively in a historiographical review of the history of Christianity in China from the 1960s to the 1990s, the field grew tremendously during the period covered by the review.[13] Researchers started out from a missiological approach and branched out to a Sinological approach. Scholars from China, Europe, and the US created a sizable body of literature in the form of chronicles, historiographical aids, editions of primary sources, and both interpretation-driven and narrative-driven histories. In the twenty years since the publication of Standaert's article, the field has remained vibrant and shows no sign of abating. The current volume of essays joins this widening stream of scholarship as a small piece in the intricate and vast puzzle of the history of Christianity in China. In fact, *Protestantism in Xiamen: Then and Now*, edited by Chris White, appeared as recently as 2019. Readers may find special interest in a chapter from this new work on Xinjie[14] Church, which was the first RCA church in Xiamen, and a chapter on the development and influence of Minnan hymns, as Stella Veenschoten of the Amoy Mission was deeply involved in Chinese church music.

Occurring within this growing body of scholarship is a quiet shift in Chinese academia and official rhetoric away from the old Party line regarding the place of the missionary movement in the history of modern China. Accusations of collusion with the forces of imperialism have not only given way to more nuanced and judicious scholarship, but they have fallen by the wayside as local governments seek to tap into the economic promises of tourism. In May 2017, the Palace Museum in Beijing opened a new gallery

---

12. Robert, "Cross-Cultural Friendship," 106.
13. Standaert, "New Trends," 573–613.
14. Formerly known as Sin-koe.

on the island of Gulangyu to exhibit its collection of Western artifacts.[15] The building that houses the gallery is the former Hope and Wilhelmina Hospital and Nursing School, which features prominently in two of the essays in this volume and is itself "a living artifact," as one of numerous articles reporting on the gallery in Chinese cyberspace points out.[16] Two months later, one of China's official news outlets Xinhuanet proudly announced that UNESCO's World Heritage Committee had decided to include the former international settlement on Gulangyu, the site of so much RCA missionary activity, "on the prestigious World Heritage List."[17] This moment was the culmination of an application process that had begun in 2008,[18] and a picture of beaming Chinese delegates accompanying the Xinhuanet announcement is evidence of this quiet change in official Chinese rhetoric. The Western presence in modern China, of which the missionary movement was an indisputably important element, is now given a place in the Chinese cultural landscape—on Chinese terms—and the present volume joins this everchanging landscape.

Bibliography

Chang, Iris. *The Rape of Nanking: The Forgotten Holocaust of World War II*. New York: Basic Books, 2009.

De Jong, Gerald F. *The Reformed Church in China, 1842–1951*. Historical Series of the Reformed Church in America, no. 22. Grand Rapids: Eerdmans, 1992.

Lu, Suping. *They Were in Nanjing: The Nanjing Massacre Witnessed by American and British Nationals*. Hong Kong: Hong Kong University Press, 2004.

Manktelow, Emily J. *Missionary Families: Race, Gender and Generation on the Spiritual Frontier*. Studies in Imperialism. Manchester: Manchester University Press, 2016.

---

15. The gallery opened its doors on May 13, 2017. Its official English name is "Kulangsu Gallery of Foreign Artifacts from the Palace Museum Collection" (故宫鼓浪屿外国文物馆); it is interesting to note that Kulangsu, the romanization by which missionaries knew the island, rather than the pinyin Gulangyu, is used here.

16. "故宫外国文物馆在鼓浪屿正式开放 Gugong waiguo wenwuguan zai Gulangyu zhengshi kaifang," 中国国情 *Zhongguo guoqing*, http://guoqing.china.com.cn/2017-05/14/content_40810019.htm (accessed September 22, 2017).

17. "China Focus: Gulangyu Island Joins UNESCO World Heritage List," *Xinhuanet*, July 8, 2017, http://news.xinhuanet.com/english/2017-07/08/c_136428637.htm (accessed September 22, 2017).

18. Deng Junfang, "Explore Gulangyu – China's 52nd UNESCO World Heritage Site," *CGTN*, July 9, 2017, https://news.cgtn.com/news/3d67444d3359444e/share_p.html (accessed September 22, 2017).

Introduction

Robert, Dana L. "Cross-Cultural Friendship in the Creation of Twentieth-Century World Christianity." *International Bulletin of Missionary Research* 35/2 (April 2011) 100–107.

Standaert, Nicolas. "New Trends in the Historiography of Christianity in China." *The Catholic Historical Review* 83/4 (1997) 573–613.

White, Chris, ed. *Protestantism in Xiamen: Then and Now*. Global Diversities. Cham, Switzerland: Springer Nature, 2019.

1

A Visionary Mission
The Life and Work of Dr. J. A. Otte

Rebekah Llorens

The study of Christian missionaries and their work enhances many different fields of inquiry. It furthers the understanding of cultural history, because missionaries have helped the spread of Christianity to both obscure and well-known peoples and lands. Missionaries have reached the far corners of the earth and have been the means for the transformation of people groups and social patterns through their message. The study of their work also enhances the life of the Church. When Christians want to know more about the history of their faith and its influence over time, the accounts of missionaries provide a time stamp for important events and developments in the spread of Christianity. An understanding of the historical role of missionaries and their strategies on the mission field may allow the missionaries of today to get a better grasp of the successes and failures of their predecessors and how they experienced them.

The life of one missionary, Dr. John A. Otte, and his service in China give insight into two realms of mission work. As a medical missionary, Otte provided healing to the Chinese people in both their bodies and their hearts. He sought to bring holistic healing without forcing his patients to become Christians. Two things are worthy of note about Otte: first, he applied his faith to his practice. For him, the work of the Gospel took priority, and medical work was simply the means to further it. Instead of forcing his patients to change their own ways to reflect Western values when they did become Christians, Otte changed his personal lifestyle to better relate to the people whom he served. Second, Otte was determined to help the Chinese remain Chinese, and not become westernized in their Christianity (that is, by living like people in Europe or North America). By adopting this cultural approach to ministry, Otte established a genuine image of the Christian faith before the Chinese people.

This study is divided into four sections. The first provides a general history of Otte and his work, giving the context for an analysis of his ministry. The second section focuses on Otte's strategy for ministering to people through his medical work. The third section analyzes the steps that Otte took to close the cultural gap and to relate to the Chinese; and the fourth summarizes the conclusions gathered from the analysis of his work.

A General History of Dr. J. A. Otte

John Abraham Otte was born on August 11, 1861, to working-class parents in Vlissenden (Flushing), the Netherlands.[1] When he was five, he and his family moved to the United States in search of a job for his father. The family settled in Grand Rapids, Michigan, and Johannes, now going by the name John, eventually attended Hope College in the city of Holland. While in school, Otte suffered several attacks of diphtheria that weakened his voice, thus destroying his mother's hope for Otte to become a minister. His weak voice and lack of interest in theology caused him to opt for medical school at the University of Michigan after graduation from Hope in 1883. It was in medical school that Otte first considered the idea of becoming a medical missionary. By this time, he had become a fervent Christian and played an important role in a revival on the campus of the University of Michigan, which was the precursor to the nationwide Student Volunteer Movement. Otte decided to approach the Reformed Church in America (RCA) about receiving support from the denomination to go to China. Most American denominations had a mission board that evaluated applicants for long-term

---

1. Frances Phelps Otte, "The Life of Dr. J. A. Otte" (unpublished manuscript, 1934), folder "Biographies about John A. Otte," John A. Otte Papers, H88–0117, Joint Archives of Holland, MI. Most information within this paragraph is found in this biography, unless otherwise noted.

missions. The RCA's Board of Foreign Missions liked his idea, but because they did not have the resources to fund him, they rejected his proposal. Instead, Otte took the suggestion of a visiting minister surnamed Van't Lindenhout to go to the Netherlands for one year to study diseases of the eye at the University of Amsterdam in Utrecht. Otte's knowledge of eye diseases would later prove useful in meeting a common need in China.[2]

While studying in the Netherlands in 1886, Dr. Otte met a little girl who inspired him. She gave Otte two Dutch halfpennies and told him to build a hospital in China with them.[3] Encouraged, Otte returned to the U.S. once his year of study was concluded and approached the RCA Board again. Although they did request that he raise more funds first, they agreed to send Otte to China. With his new wife, Frances Phelps (daughter of Philip Phelps, Hope College's first president), and with funding from supporters, Otte set out for China in 1887, arriving there in January 1888.[4]

Otte set his mind to building a hospital, which he did both quickly and efficiently. In the village of Xiaoxi (referred to as Sio-khe by RCA missionaries of the time) in Fujian province, he established Neerbosch Hospital, named after the orphanage founded by Mr. Van't Lindenhout in the Netherlands. Otte completed this project within the first year of his arrival in China, but not without resistance from local villagers. The Chinese considered the area on which he planned to build the hospital sacred ground, and many tried to sabotage his efforts. Otte persisted through these obstacles, and his efforts bore fruit from the first night of the hospital's opening. Local inhabitants flooded the hospital and began to learn what the foreign doctor could offer them. From tumor removal surgeries to eye surgeries to amputations, Otte quickly began to deliver relief to a longsuffering people and to establish his ministry.[5]

In 1897, after a two-year furlough, Otte returned to China with the goal of building a hospital in Xiamen (referred to as Amoy by RCA

---

2. Van Nes, *Dr. J. A. Otte, Zendeling-Arts in China*; English translation by Walter de Velder, "Beams of Light upon the Field of the World (Dr. J. A. Otte)," 3, folder "Biographies about John A. Otte," John A. Otte Papers.

3. According to the conversion calculator on DutchAncestryCoach.com, the 2 halfpennies equaled about 70 percent of a day's wages for an unskilled worker in 1886 and convert to a little over 60 dollars in today's U.S. dollars.

4. Warnshuis, "A Brief Sketch" (unpublished manuscript, 1911), 10, folder "Biographies about John A. Otte."

5. Warnshuis, "A Brief Sketch," 11–12, which quotes from a pamphlet by Dr. Otte, "The Healing Art in China."

missionaries of the time), the city where the RCA's China mission first began. He set his sights on the island of Gulangyu (referred to as Kulangsu by RCA missionaries of the time), across a small body of water from the island of Xiamen.[6] This time, Otte met resistance not from local Chinese, but from other foreign settlers. Many feared the danger of close proximity to foreign diseases, while others were concerned about a potential rise in property costs. Soon enough, Otte's efforts overcame their protests as well, and he completed Hope Hospital in 1896 and later built alongside it a women's hospital, which was subsequently renamed Wilhelmina Hospital.[7] These names came from Hope College, Dr. and Mrs. Otte's alma mater, and from the queen of the Netherlands, a generous benefactor of the institution, respectively. In due course, these hospitals, also jointly known as the Hope and Wilhelmina Hospital, served both the Chinese and the foreign populations of Xiamen, Gulangyu, and the inland regions.

Each day spent doing medical mission work was full. In addition to his medical work, Otte initially served as the head administrator of the hospital. As the number of Chinese Christians grew, he handed the position over to one of them; but he did not cease to make house calls and perform operations, always speaking the truth of salvation to his patients as he interacted with them. The time spent in person-to-person interactions was balanced with the time Otte took to write articles for numerous mission and RCA journals. He included counts of patients, stories of both mundane and miraculous healings, and requests for prayer in these often-extensive accounts. He sent one every few days to one of a number of periodicals to which he was a regular contributor. Without these writings, many details about Otte's work and mission would not be known today.

The full schedule that marked Otte's ministry was seen even during furloughs. While his family stayed in one place, Otte frequently traveled on speaking tours both in the U.S. and in the Netherlands to raise funds from supporters.[8] He shared stories of conversions, inspiration, and hope about the work in China, which excited his listeners. Otte made sure to bring

---

6. De Jong, *The Reformed Church in China*, 160.

7. The original name of the women's hospital was Netherlands Women's Hospital, but was changed to Wilhelmina Hospital in 1904 when Queen Wilhelmina of the Netherlands agreed to be named "Protectress," or principal benefactor, of the institution. Wilhelmina Hospital is the name used in this research because it is most consistent with and most reflective of the Dutch nation's desire to stay involved in Otte's mission work. See Warnshuis, "A Brief Sketch," 18, 20.

8. Warnshuis, "A Brief Sketch," 17, 19.

along the two Dutch half-pennies which he had encased in gold and strung on a chain as a meaningful illustration for himself and for his audiences. Donations and volunteers for the field multiplied in response to Otte's presentations. Hope and Neerbosch hospitals eventually became self-sufficient (meaning that only the missionary doctors received financial support from the Board, and the Netherlanders insisted on supporting Wilhelmina Hospital), but financial support helped, and prayer support was always necessary. The RCA ordained Otte during his first furlough so that he might actively participate in the leadership meetings of the Chinese church.[9] The ordination was a recognition of the work of the Reverend Doctor Otte as both a spiritual and a medical minister to the Chinese people.

In April 1910, Otte responded to a house call for a man dangerously ill with pneumonic plague. Within a few days, Otte himself began to display signs of the illness, eventually becoming bedridden with chills and aching joints. He weakened further and died on April 14, 1910, at the age of 49. His wife, Frances, who was back in the United States for their children's schooling, received notice as quickly as his colleagues could send it, and his friends buried him in China. Two pastors conducted the service in English and Chinese, and Otte's Chinese friends erected a memorial next to Hope and Wilhelmina Hospital with inscriptions in English, Chinese, Dutch, and Latin.[10] Chinese and Westerners alike gathered for the funeral, a living testimony to his work among both people groups.

Dr. John A. Otte: Missionary before Medical Doctor

The desire to spread the glory of God motivated Otte more than anything else. In his mind, the purpose of the hospitals was first for the spread of the Gospel, and second for medical recovery. He did not want to carry out "medical work and also missionary work as a concomitant."[11] Otte experienced different encounters with healing in his practice, and through it all, he centered his work on Christ. When he went on speaking tours or wrote reports, he consistently requested prayer as the most essential support for the ministry.[12] Otte's hope for the Chinese people did not consist in chang-

---

9. Warnshuis, "A Brief Sketch," 19.

10. De Velder, "Beams of Light," 1.

11. Frances Phelps Otte, "The Life of Dr. J. A. Otte," 11, quoting from a certain Dr. Van Staveren.

12. Otte and his wife regularly contributed articles about their mission work to a

ing them into Westerners, but in welcoming the Holy Spirit to bring their culture to a better version of itself. Otte mourned the suffering and injustice in Chinese society, believing that "There is but one thing necessary to make of China a grand nation, and that is the religion of the Lord Jesus."[13] Therefore, the Ottes frequently asked for prayer from their supporters for the Chinese people, and for the "one, true, pure, *Holy* Spirit. . .to become an abiding presence in their hearts and homes and very lives."[14] The transformation and conversion of hearts the Ottes prayed for often happened because of successful surgeries and other medical procedures. Out of all the successes that Dr. Otte had, the exposure of the Chinese patients to the Christian Gospel made him "happier than anything else."[15] Serving God and helping others come to worship him was the principal goal of Otte's work.

To achieve this end, Otte sought to establish hospitals as places of faith and Christ-centered relief. Before giving treatment, Otte required patients to hear a Bible lesson.[16] A decision for conversion was not necessary, but he wanted each patient to have the opportunity to hear the Gospel. Rarely would a person choose not to hear the lesson, but in such a case, the hospital would charge "thirty cash."[17] Most patients chose to hear the lesson, and if there were complaints about the policy, Dr. Otte did not feel the need to write about them in his articles or letters.[18] After that stage followed the

---

number of Christian periodicals, most of which no longer exist. Typescripts of these articles, published or intended for publication and often without complete publication information, are found in the folder "Articles—Foreign Missions, 1886-1949," John A. Otte Papers. For example, one of Dr. Otte's articles, titled "Hospital Work Enlarged," in which he asked his readers for prayer support, was published sometime in August 1906, but the periodical in which it appeared is not known.

13. John A. Otte, "Conditions at Amoy," periodical title unknown, 28 August 1900, folder "Articles—Foreign Missions, 1886-1949," John A. Otte Papers.

14. Frances Phelps Otte, incomplete typescript of an article published in *Mission Gleaner*, issue and date unknown, folder "Articles—Foreign Missions, 1886-1949."

15. John A. Otte to Rev. Peter Moerdyke, reprinted in a newspaper published in Grand Rapids, Michigan, sometime in 1889, name of newspaper and date unknown, folder "Articles—Foreign Missions, 1886-1949."

16. Reformed Church in America, "Amoy District," *Seventieth Annual Report*, 7-9.

17. Reformed Church in America, "Amoy District," *Seventieth Annual Report*, 7-9. The Chinese cash, or *wen*, was a currency denomination used from the imperial times to the early twentieth century. One *wen* was a thousandth of a *yuan*; hence the amount of 30 cash was not meant to be a real barrier to those seeking medical assistance.

18. De Velder, "Beams of Light," 5-6.

direct contact that Otte had with patients as he treated them. He enjoyed sharing the "words of life and love of a redeeming Savior" with those he met, supervising the overall spiritual life of the hospital while attending to his medical and administrative duties.[19] Sharing the Gospel was an integral part of Otte's medical ministry and a comfort to his patients.

Otte did his best to take care of the sick and to share Jesus with them, but he understood that some might hear the Word better from their own people than from a foreigner. To this end, Otte welcomed native evangelists into the hospital. These evangelists eventually took over most of Otte's duties as overseer of the Gospel work.[20] Many of the native evangelists working with Otte had been converted at the hospital through healing, but others stayed because they wanted fellow patients to know the Gospel, regardless of the outcomes of the medical treatments they had received. On one occasion, Otte's wife, Frances, took note of an elderly woman, who was sickly herself, ministering to the hospital's patients.[21] Otte frequently mentioned in his reports the leadership of a matron, Eng-sui, and two blind evangelists who worked in the hospital.[22] One might reasonably surmise that the two blind men had originally come for treatment but had not been healed. If that was indeed the case, then faith in Jesus would have been the deciding factor that kept them there despite their disappointed hopes for physical healing.

While the administration of the hospital was Otte's "official" work, his policies for his medical practice reflected his desire to reach people with the Gospel. The American doctor did not refuse treatment to people, whether Christian or non-Christian, native or foreign. The only charge for admission he required was the cost of food from those who could afford it. Although Otte did charge the thirty cash for refusing the Bible lesson prior to treatment, no further commitment by the patient was necessary. For those interested in Christianity, opportunities to learn more were available.[23] The pattern seemed to be that patients became Christians later, more because of the medical work than because of the Gospel message they heard before

19. P. W. Pitcher, "In Memoriam," *The Christian Intelligencer*, 22 June 1910, 396.

20. John A. Otte, "Dr. Otte at Work Again," 1 May 1905, periodical unknown, folder "Articles—Foreign Missions, 1886–1949."

21. Frances Phelps Otte, incomplete typescript of an article published in *Mission Gleaner*.

22. John A. Otte, "Dr. Otte at Work Again."

23. These resources included the native evangelists, daily hearing of the Bible, and the like.

receiving treatment. Otte's medical training had prepared him to take care of problems for which traditional Chinese medicine had no solution: tumors, hygienic amputations, and diseases of the eye.[24] The goal of "making the blind see," as the biblical phrase puts it, encouraged Otte in his work as he tried to tend to the bodily needs of the Chinese in conjunction with their spiritual needs.[25] If Otte succeeded in making a patient well in an "easy" case, he credited his talent to God; and when he could not make a patient well, he led the person to pray to God for healing. This became his method for the more difficult cases, and it was the approach Otte adopted during much of his early work while trying to develop a relationship with the Chinese people. Frances Otte put it thus: "During the first years, if a death had occurred, it would humanly speaking have been fatal to the cause. The natives did not learn any too quickly to trust the Christians either foreign or Chinese. Providence mercifully spared lives when all human skill seemed unavailing and nothing but earnest prayer carried through a seemingly hopeless patient."[26]

Times like these tested the true caliber of Otte's mission, and his personal dependence on God taught his Chinese patients to follow his example when medicine reached its limits. Nevertheless, the wide range of responses from Otte's patients indicates that his work was not as easy as a one-time acceptance of the Gospel, no matter what level of treatment they received. One woman needed to hear the Gospel twice. She attempted suicide after her first visit to the hospital but was rescued and brought back. Only during her second stint in the hospital did she turn to Christ.[27] Others received treatment but never became believers at all, and the people who saw the healing of their loved ones did not necessarily convert either. During one house call, Otte treated a person in the house and met a woman who lived there with the patient. He spoke to her, telling her that she was "so full of kindness" to welcome him into her home and to care so well for the patient, but that he wanted to see her in heaven someday. Unconvinced, the only response she gave Otte was a smile.[28] In some cases of wealthy

---

24. Frances Phelps Otte, "The Life of Dr. J. A. Otte," 6–7.

25. John A. Otte, "The Corner-Stone Laid," 25 October 1886, unknown newspaper, folder "Articles—Foreign Missions, 1886–1949."

26. Frances Phelps Otte, "The Life of Dr. J. A. Otte," 7.

27. John A. Otte, clipping of an article that was first published in *Mission Gleaner* on 3 April 1910, folder "Articles—Foreign Missions, 1886–1949."

28. John A. Otte, untitled article printed in *Mission Gleaner*, 6 April 1910.

patients, Otte did not always witness their conversions (that is, his papers do not always specify this fact), but he often noticed a change of heart in them after treatment. The immediate fruit that came from Otte's ministry to them often consisted of spontaneous financial gifts to the hospital. Gifts of four thousand guilders, twelve hundred guilders for electricity in the hospital, and a motor boat for transport to make house calls all came from rich patients who desired to further the doctor's work.[29] If these gifts had been motivated by spiritual conviction, Otte did not always know it, given his silence on the matter with regard to these gifts. Nonetheless, these gifts speak to the power and deeper purpose of Otte's work. Even though he did not always witness his preferred response of conversion to Christ, he persisted in his work; and the wealthy noticed the positive changes that Otte brought to the people with whom he interacted. Regardless of whether they desired to give for spiritual purposes, no one can deny the importance that they placed on Otte's work when they decided to help him financially.

Otte's methods to establish a Christian atmosphere in his hospital and bring the Chinese people to faith by means of medical work were relatively new to the RCA, and they established a pattern for winning hearts and souls in a mission field, which would be followed by others. The efficacy and importance of the Gospel in medical missions were also reflected in the work of another medical missionary from a different denomination, Dr. L. Nelson Bell, who began his missionary career about six years after Otte's death, and who was to become the father-in-law of the famous American evangelist Billy Graham. Dr. Bell was sent to Qingjiangpu[30] in northern Jiangsu[31] province by the Presbyterian Church in the United States (popularly known as the Southern Presbyterian Church).[32] The overarching belief that Bell held was the same as Otte's: the health of the soul was the first priority for his work. Someone said of him, "Dr. Bell saw every patient as in need of bodily healing but also in need of the grace of God in Christ. He was happy when he could say, 'Take up thy bed and walk'; but he never felt that his work was fully done until he could add, 'My son, thy sins are forgiven thee.'"[33] Indeed, while medicine was his means of reaching the Chinese people, Bell asked supporters in the U.S. to give their prayers first,

29. De Velder, "Beams of Light," 14.
30. Spelled Tsingkiangpu formerly.
31. Spelled Kiangsu formerly.
32. Pollock, *A Foreign Devil in China*, 36.
33. Pollock, *A Foreign Devil in China*, 79.

calling prayer "the greatest thing" that they could give to the ministry.[34] In the same spirit, Bell sought to make the hospital a place of Christian healing and faith. He wrote a pamphlet in Chinese, titled "Words of Eternal Life," which outlined the Gospel message for new patients at the hospital. By providing this pamphlet for free to all patients and making sure that every patient was contacted by another Chinese believer to connect him or her with a local church, Bell helped establish the groundwork for a great Christian movement.[35]

Unlike Otte, however, Bell entered the system of a well-established hospital called Love-and-Mercy Hospital in Qingjiangpu. Bell arrived at the young age of twenty-two but in eighteen months took over as superintendent of the hospital when the veteran missionary doctor took his furlough.[36] As head of the establishment, Bell quickly gained experience in areas in which he had had little or no prior training—in his case, in diseases of the eye. Bell performed his first cataract surgery from memory. While he had never done the surgery, Bell remembered watching professors do it in the United States, and he successfully executed it. From the spread of the good news after the surgery, Bell became known as the doctor who could "make the blind to see."[37] While the reputation of his surgical abilities spread in China, his greatest joy was still helping the Chinese to learn about Christ. Bell wrote in a letter to a ministry supporter, "Hand in hand with this work has been personal presentation of Jesus to these patients and *that* is what really brings the personal joy to this work."[38] This letter points to the true motivation for and meaning of Bell's work: the winning of souls for God.

Whether or not Bell had heard of Otte or studied his methods, medical or missional, is not known, but the idea that the work in the body would open the soul is prevalent in both doctors' ministries. The personal letters and denominational reports of both men indicate this in successful medical cases. What about those cases in which nothing could be done? In these, Bell carried on in the consistent faith that Otte shared; when nothing more

---

34. Bell to "My dear Friends" (possibly to old fraternity friends of Omega Upsilon Phi, the medical fraternity to which Bell belonged), 21 January 1927, folder 1, box 1, collection 318 Papers of Lemuel Nelson Bell, Archives of the Billy Graham Center, Wheaton, Illinois.

35. Pollock, *A Foreign Devil in China*, 77.

36. Pollock, *A Foreign Devil in China*, 47.

37. Pollock, *A Foreign Devil in China*, 49.

38. Bell to Benjamin Clayton, 27 September 1936, folder 9, box 1, collection 318 Papers of Lemuel Nelson Bell. Emphasis in the original.

could be done, both doctors pointed the patient and his or her family to God. An excerpt from one of Bell's letters illustrates the missionary doctor's honesty to his ministry supporters, while providing evidence that in his eyes, ultimate blessing came from spiritual work:

> After reading of these cases you may say—what a wonderful place, all the patients get well. No; I am sorry to say they do not. Three died here in one day recently and we have many disappointments and failures. But—the successes so outnumber the failures that I like to tell you of them. You may be surprised to hear tho that sometimes we seem to do more good, from a spiritual standpoint, in those cases in which we fail to relieve the body. The friends and relatives may be won by what we do for their loved ones.[39]

Not everything went smoothly or ideally in the medical sphere, but this did not hinder Bell from taking the opportunity to win the patient's family through his actions and "loving interest in each case," which often made a deep impact on them.[40] This was the spirit in which Otte had pioneered medical work in the Amoy Mission, and Bell's story shows the continued effectiveness of the strategy of prioritizing spiritual goals even in medical missions in the twentieth century.

If Otte ever encountered an obstacle that challenged his body-to-heart approach for success, it was opium. British traders introduced opium to China in the early eighteenth century, and by the time of Otte's ministry the trade had expanded into a dependency problem for the Chinese people. The Chinese government recognized the negative effects of opium and in the early 1800s banned it, except for "medicinal" purposes. By then, however, the culture had adopted opium smoking as a recreational activity.[41] When approaching the problem of opium addiction, Otte observed that most addicts actually needed the opposite of his typical approach. Those that became addicted to opium were, as Otte described them, "slaves of the soul-destroying habit," and little progress could be made by human will or medical effort alone.[42] The most complete break from addiction resulted

---

39. Bell to "Friends," 4 July 1929, folder 2, box 1, collection 318 Papers of Lemuel Nelson Bell.
40. Pollock, *A Foreign Devil in China*, 49.
41. Spence, *The Search for Modern China* (3rd ed.), 127–130.
42. John A. Otte, article or letter (about the mission work in Xiaoxi) printed in an unknown newspaper, 29 December 1890, folder "Articles—Foreign Missions, 1886–1949," John A. Otte Papers.

after the individual placed his or her faith in Christ. For one particular group of patients at Neerbosch Hospital, Otte noted that once they became Christians, "not one of them ... returned to the habit."[43] Chinese addicts eventually came to understand the strength of the substance; but, more importantly, some among them grasped the power of the solution that Otte offered, and the impact it could have on their people. As a result, one response of the wealthier Chinese to Otte's ministry was financial gifts for an opium ward, which aided many more addicts in their recovery.[44] The approach may have needed adjustment, but the goal was still the same for Otte. A heart won for Christ, in this case, proved doubly helpful for the complete healing of a patient.

The most effective way in which Otte carried on spreading the Gospel was through his medical students. Almost as soon as he established a hospital, Otte began to find Chinese Christian youths eager to begin medical training. He only accepted Christian students in the hope that they would use their ability in the same venue he did: healing both the body and the spirit in Christ.[45] These students took classes from Otte and practiced their skills in the hospital alongside him. At first, the number of students was small, as only one of Otte's then four medical students came with him from Neerbosch Hospital in Xiaoxi to establish Hope Hospital in Xiamen; but in the following years he had as many as twenty male and female students a year.[46]

Some might argue that Otte, Bell, and other medical missionaries like them traded their medical services for the "Christianizing" of the Chinese people, to add to the count of converts that they had. While some may have approached the mission field as an area to conquer, Otte viewed the Chinese people as in need of help but also as having great medical and spiritual potential. He did require patients to hear readings from the Bible every day, but there did not seem to be any resistance to this from the patients themselves.[47] Otte did not force a decision for Christ, as evidenced by the number of stories that do not describe an obvious conversion. On the

---

43. John A. Otte, article or letter (about the mission work in Xiaoxi) printed in an unknown newspaper, 29 December 1890.

44. John A. Otte, article or letter (about the mission work in Xiaoxi) printed in an unknown newspaper, 29 December 1890.

45. Warnshuis, "A Brief Sketch," 27.

46. Frances Phelps Otte, "The Life of Dr. J. A. Otte," 10.

47. Van Nes, *Dr. J. A. Otte, Zendeling-Arts in China*, 5–6.

other hand, the treatment of people addicted to opium revealed the level of spiritual interest from the patients, because complete healing consistently came with a genuine desire for Christ. Otte had to wrestle with the physical and the spiritual as he did his best, noting, "It is scarcely possible to save an opium smoker unless he becomes a Christian. This is a fearful curse, which overshadows China like a cloud, and which is leading its millions of victims to moral, intellectual, and spiritual ruin, and to an untimely grave."[48] In the case of opium addicts, the decision to become a Christian was necessary, but as indicated in Otte's account, the doctor was powerless until the patient made the decision of his or her own accord.

Otte was a doctor with a variety of talents useful in mission work: he was a good surgeon, a personable manager, and a passionate follower of Christ. A nurse named Marie Kranenburg, who traveled to China to join Otte at his hospital, observed, "I am astonished at what Dr. Otte has to do. He operates, visits all the wards, treats the patients, holds clinics, teaches students, and busies himself with accounts in order to make the limited funds go as far as possible. He hurries with the conveyance to his plague patients. He preaches, builds schools, and is now enlarging the hospital."[49] Despite the wide range of jobs that Otte needed to do, he did his best to relate to his patients and help them make the connection between the healing of their bodies and the healing of their hearts in God. This aspect of his work made him effective for Christ in tangible ways that greatly affected and expanded the Chinese Church.

Dr. John A. Otte: A Missionary's Struggle for Cultural Understanding

Whereas Otte was the first RCA medical missionary to go to China, he was, however, not the first missionary to reside in a different culture, and certainly not the first to wrestle with differences between his home culture and the culture in which he ministered. From the beginning of mission work, as narrated in the book of Acts in the New Testament, the Apostle Paul struggled between being a Jew and reaching Gentiles.[50] Ever since

---

48. [John A. Otte], untitled article printed in *The Mission Field* (possibly 1888), folder "Articles—Foreign Missions, 1886–1949."

49. "A Digest of the Biography of Dr. J. A. Otte Published Recently in the Netherlands," 9, folder "Biographies about John A. Otte—Unpublished Manuscripts, n.d., 1910–1935."

50. The book of Acts contains multiple accounts of the struggle of Paul, a Jew, to

that time, missionaries have wrestled with the best application of the Bible and its guidelines for the Christian life, especially when relating to other cultures. Some missionaries set requirements that converts had to meet before acquiring church membership; in fact, RCA missionaries in particular were known for their strict regulations for church membership.[51] Nonetheless, some missionaries decided to adapt as much as they could to Chinese culture by affirming it rather than altering it to resemble their own. Otte believed in the potential of the culture to worship the Christian God in a specifically Chinese way, eventually without the help of missionaries or foreign support. By learning more about Chinese culture, changing his approach to cross class and gender divisions, and designing his work in the mission hospitals to help them become financially and spiritually self-sustaining, Otte allowed the Chinese people to accept Christianity in their cultural context, without giving up those practices of theirs that did not conflict with the Bible's teachings.

Otte first demonstrated his goal to reach the Chinese people most effectively for Christ by overcoming the cultural barriers that confronted him personally, including the communication gap and the distrust of the people. Most missionaries during the nineteenth century reached China with no knowledge of the Chinese language, and so they usually spent the first year or two studying it before beginning actual mission work. When Otte arrived in China, he took the time early in his career to do so.[52] His commitment to language study enabled him to connect with the local inhabitants personally, rather than through an interpreter or hand gestures and body language. Otte's willingness to learn their language revealed his desire to embrace them as a people with their own heritage.

In addition to the language difference, missionaries often faced hostility from the Chinese. In Otte's experience, his reception on arrival was so cold that he believed "the people would have murdered us had they dared to do so," and the likelihood of bonding with the people seemed rather slim in the early months of his ministry.[53] While chances for improved relations increased over time in part because Otte displayed consistency and fairness

relate to Gentiles, a term used by Jews for non-Jewish peoples. For example, Acts 17 has an account of Paul speaking to Athenians and making the connection between an aspect of their polytheistic views and the Gospel message.

51. De Jong, *The Reformed Church in China*, 40–45.
52. Warnshuis, "A Brief Sketch," 10.
53. John A. Otte, "Letter to Parents from Sio-khe, China," unknown Grand Rapids newspaper, 6 Januanry 1895, folder "Articles—Foreign Missions, 1886–1949."

in his medical work, a more important factor that strengthened the bond between the Western missionary and local Chinese was the hospitality of the Otte family. The family kept their door open to anyone who needed them and often hosted Chinese neighbors for dinner and Bible study. People came to trust Otte because he was honest and openly shared one of his resources that Chinese society valued highly: his home.

As soon as he became more comfortable in the foreign setting, Otte began to feel the barriers within the Chinese culture itself that prevented him from reaching the masses with the Gospel. The most difficult hurdle for Otte to overcome in his ministry was the structure of social classes. Each class had its set of problems and complaints with Christianity, and Otte wrestled with the best approach to use for bringing the most people from each social class to Christ. Otte began to realize that working with the wealthy required the most care. Whenever he tried to share his faith with the upper classes, he had to follow cultural protocol to stay in their good graces for fear of being "considered as lacking in taste and etiquette, and quite regardless of 'good form.'"[54] This protocol included lighting fireworks when Chinese officials entered the church and providing a dividing screen in a room of mixed classes.[55] In a letter to the *Mission Gleaner*, a periodical published by the denomination that sent the Ottes to China, the doctor described the delicate balance in approaching the wealthy. A Christian who received an invitation to a higher-class home could not display too much enthusiasm for the Gospel, for fear of offending the host; but if the Christian guest did not broach the subject of faith, then it was unlikely that the host would take the step to come to church on his own.[56] Otte struggled to find the best approach to the wealthy, but sometimes the response of the poor to the Gospel did not encourage him either. On one occasion, Otte arrived in a town for a house call and saw the chapel completely deserted because the townspeople had stopped gathering there. When asked why, the people replied that Christianity seemed "unsuited to the needs of people so poor as the Chinese," a point that he tried to counter. However, he found that he could not always satisfy the listener.[57]

---

54. Frances Phelps Otte, "At Home and Abroad," (most likely) *Mission Gleaner*, (possibly) April 1898, folder "Articles—Foreign Missions, 1886–1949."

55. Frances Phelps Otte, "At Home and Abroad," (most likely) *Mission Gleaner*, (possibly) April 1898.

56. John A. Otte, untitled article, *Mission Gleaner*, 6 April 1910, folder "Articles—Foreign Missions, 1886–1949."

57. [John A. Otte], article of unknown title, printed in unknown periodical, April

Another challenge that Otte encountered in his mission work was gender. Men acted freely in Chinese society much as they did in Western society, but women stayed separate from men as a rule, often with dividing screens at mixed-gender gatherings. The division ran so deep that for the first few months at Neerbosch Hospital, Otte did not treat any Chinese women. When at last a woman came to receive treatment, some Chinese Christians and the missionaries prayed over her together, and she was healed. Had the woman died, the missionaries thought the local Chinese would have had an excuse to keep their women from treatment.[58] While Otte did not often mention the difficulty of reaching the women of Chinese society, he did specifically establish Wilhelmina Hospital for the treatment of women and wrote to the RCA requesting a nurse assistant from the United States to teach midwifery to Chinese women.[59] Chinese society prevented men from treating women, a tradition that caused a gap between capable healers and women in labor. If Dr. Otte had failed to respect this aspect of Chinese culture and refused to empower the Chinese, he would not have made the request. Instead, he chose to bring a Western *woman* to *teach Chinese women*—a point of connection that allowed Chinese women the opportunity to study medicine, while giving Chinese women improved care during childbirth and respecting their cultural tradition.

The cultural hurdles that Otte confronted caused difficulty in everyday interactions with the Chinese, but the medical work he did was successful in part because of his cultural sensitivity. From the beginning of Hope Hospital, in particular, Otte sought to make the atmosphere one in which the Chinese patients felt as comfortable as possible. For instance, instead of the metal-spring beds that Western hospitals typically used, he insisted on using wooden boards for the beds, complete with wooden or bamboo pillows, in the traditional Chinese style.[60] He also designed the hospital's kitchen in a style familiar to Chinese cooks, making sure to include all the "peculiar Chinese cooking arrangements" so that Chinese meals could be prepared for patients.[61] These steps allowed for a more comfortable setting for the patients. To create an atmosphere in the hospital that was conducive

1892, folder "Articles—Foreign Missions, 1886–1949."

58. Warnshuis, "A Brief Sketch," 12, quoting from Dr. Otte's pamphlet "The Healing Art in China."

59. Van Nes, *Dr. J. A. Otte, Zendeling-Arts in China*, 11.

60. Warnshuis, "A Brief Sketch," 25.

61. Frances Phelps Otte, "At Home and Abroad."

to conversations on spiritual matters, he invited many Chinese Christians to become evangelists in the hospital to reach different groups of people. Chinese Christian medical students also shared the Word of God with the patients they met, which made the Chinese voice prominent in the spread of the Christian faith in the hospital.[62] Consequently, upon leaving the hospital, new converts went out to different towns and expanded and stabilized local congregations, enabling them to become self-sufficient.[63]

While the spiritual atmosphere of the hospital encouraged Chinese Christians and new converts to apply their faith to their life situations, the financial management of the hospital kept the Chinese believers from becoming dependent on foreign assistance. Otte had begun his work with funding from friends in the Netherlands and the United States. When on furlough, he devoted much time to trips to raise funds and "promote interest in the work at Amoy," and the construction of all three hospitals of the RCA's Amoy Mission was paid for by the funds Otte raised.[64] Even as he carried out this work, Otte envisioned a day when these trips would no longer be necessary for the hospitals' continued existence. In due course, Otte needed less and less help from donors back home. Just before he died, only Wilhelmina Hospital still received financial support from the Dutch community, and as for the funding of the other hospitals, "none of it [came] from America."[65] Otte's desire for the financial independence of the hospitals was so strong that it worried the board members of the RCA. According to those at home, Otte seemed to be "in too great a measure seeking independence and self-support," both in ministry style and financial management.[66] Independence, while perhaps a point of tension between Otte and the Board, undoubtedly strengthened the Chinese people and their involvement in taking responsibility for the hospitals and the spiritual work that they fostered. With the support of the people, the ministry grew deeper roots than it could have done had the hospitals remained solely in the hands of a foreigner. Meanwhile, the physical and spiritual healing that

---

62. Warnshuis, "A Brief Sketch," 26.

63. Warnshuis, "A Brief Sketch," 14.

64. [John A. Otte] to unknown recipient, date unknown, February 1904, folder "Correspondence—Unaddressed, 1893–1910," John A. Otte Papers.

65. [John A. Otte] to unknown recipient, date unknown, February 1910, folder "Correspondence—Unaddressed, 1893–1910."

66. Van Nes, *Dr. J. A. Otte, Zendeling-Arts in China*, 9.

Otte offered gradually gained him credibility in the eyes of the Chinese community.

Missionaries who arrived after Otte also saw the need for the Chinese people to take Christianity and the various works associated with it into their own hands. Dr. Nelson Bell, who reached China in 1916, worked from that conviction and established the policies of Love-and-Mercy Hospital on that principle. Though he was not the founder of the hospital, Bell received the reins of leadership quickly once his predecessor took furlough, and he handled the position of principal administrator well.[67] He sought to bring in Chinese leadership wherever possible and avoided overdependence on Western money.[68] This efficient management and incorporation of Chinese responsibility proved itself in 1927 when Bell and his family had to leave China because of the Northern Expedition.[69]

During the time when Bell and his family were in the United States, Chinese believers proved that they could keep the hospital in operation in the absence of the missionary. They did so for twenty months until the Bells' return in December 1928.[70] The Chinese staff welcomed the Bell family's return enthusiastically and presented an impressive report of the hospital's affairs. Two Chinese physicians, Dr. Ts'ao and Dr. Ch'ien, had kept track of the finances,[71] including paying all the bills and maintaining reasonable prices for treatment. Almost as soon as he returned to Qingjiangpu, Bell wrote a letter to a fellow missionary relating how the hospital had fared in his absence. Among the noteworthy details Bell included was a statement of one Chinese worker at the hospital (possibly one of the physicians) about the hospital's finances: "We may have been unwise in the use of some of the money but I know it has come and gone honestly."[72] One local man stated that the hospital was the only trustworthy establishment in the area because of its honest management.[73] In spite of difficult circumstances, the Chinese

---

67. Pollock, *A Foreign Devil in China*, 47.

68. Pollock, *A Foreign Devil in China*, 76.

69. Military expedition (1926–28) jointly undertaken by Nationalist and Communist forces to defeat the warlords in central and northern China. It led to the establishment of the Guomindang regime in Nanjing in 1928.

70. Pollock, *A Foreign Devil in China*, 103–105.

71. Pollock, *A Foreign Devil in China*, 104.

72. Lemuel Nelson Bell to Mr. Woods, 26 December 1928, box 1, folder 1, collection 318 Papers of Lemuel Nelson Bell.

73. Lemuel Nelson Bell to Mr. Woods, 26 December 1928.

people clung to the tradition that Bell had created, and they demonstrated the skills for managing the facility as he had taught them.

For both Otte and Bell, discretion was necessary to decide when the gradual break from Western support would occur. Obviously, the RCA voiced its misgivings about Otte's independence and desire to help the Chinese achieve self-sufficiency as Christians and hospital workers. Bell had his own reservations about giving complete control to the Chinese staff of Love-and-Mercy Hospital. He recognized that the Chinese people could manage well enough on their own for a while, but in the end, they seemed to do better under Western leadership in times of crisis.[74] While this might seem contradictory, Bell only held this view with respect to Western institutions (like hospitals), not with respect to Chinese churches. He believed that "to keep a church subsidized from foreign funds was to keep it weak," but he also noticed that, on his return from the evacuation of 1927, with respect to the hospital, the Chinese workers were "only too thankful" to see him again.[75] This delicate balance caused controversy for missionaries of the time, but Otte and Bell did what they could to support, and not cripple, Chinese Christians. Here, too, the doctors fought for the Chinese people's identification with Christianity as a faith, and not Westernization as a way of life.

In expressing both personal care and public concern, Otte did his best to help the Chinese people understand the Christian faith as something more than the practices and traditions of the West. He devoted himself to his mission work with the ultimate goal of helping Chinese Christians take hold of the work, even if it was hard to see when that aspiration would become a reality. Otte's independence may have worried his mission board, but his spirit undoubtedly encouraged the Chinese staff of Hope and Wilhelmina Hospital to take the next step in managing the hospital and spreading the Gospel. He did his part to make sure that someday, "all nations and tongues will be gathered around the table of our common Lord,"[76] including Western people and Chinese people, representing their distinct cultures to God's glory.

---

74. Pollock, *A Foreign Devil in China*, 142.

75. Pollock, *A Foreign Devil in China*, 142.

76. John A. Otte, "A Native Pastor's Thirty Years' Anniversary," unknown periodical, unknown date (most likely 1889), folder "Articles—Foreign Missions, 1886–1949," John A. Otte Papers.

Conclusion

The life of Dr. John A. Otte is a fascinating study of mission purpose and strategy. From the beginning of his time in China, Otte desired to serve God first, a perspective that proved incredibly powerful. He used his medical skill to heal the bodies of the Chinese people so that they might see a glimpse of the Great Physician, Jesus Christ. As Otte established hospitals one after another, he gave priority to the spiritual healing aspect of his work without forcing his patients to convert to Christianity. By demonstrating love to them with both his words and his actions, Otte gained their trust in personal relationships. Then, when his medical abilities could not help anymore, he pointed to God as the ultimate Healer and Redeemer. Numerous Chinese became Christians because of Otte's insistence that his abilities came from God and his unwavering belief that his patients could be healed holistically in Him. Personal relationships with the Chinese people allowed Otte to connect with them and to show them the kind of relationship that they could have with their heavenly Father.

In leading Chinese to Christ, at no point did Otte force the new Christians to abandon their cultural practices for his. Rather, he allowed them to keep those things that were not essential to salvation—cuisine, dress, and so on—as the unique part of their Chinese identity. Otte healed the people in the best way he knew medically and physically, but this approach did not come at the expense of their culture. Sometimes becoming a Christian actually allowed his patients to heal better physically. While conversion to Christianity was often life-changing, Otte watched the change that the faith made in new Christians without dictating the behaviors of individual converts. As a result, the ministry expanded, and Chinese Christians became actively involved in the work. They were enabled to lead because of the guidance and support that Otte gave them.

Bell's ministry at a later time and in a different location confirmed Otte's approach to medicine as a key to the human heart. He used many of Otte's strategies, including evangelism in the hospital and training Chinese staff to run the work themselves. Like Otte before him, Bell created an environment in the hospital that encouraged spiritual inquiry and prepared Chinese believers to reach their own people with the Gospel. Bell may have had concerns about giving them complete ownership of the hospital facility, but he did his best to empower them to play an active role in the ministry of healing. Thus, Bell's work echoed Otte's goal of eventual Chinese leadership.

This study of Otte's mission work reveals the importance of different cultures to Christianity, and the powerful impact of keeping new Christians in their cultural setting. The new converts had the ability to "go where [the missionary] cannot, and reach those who are entirely beyond [the missionary's] influence."[77] Cultural differences can be a real obstacle in effective evangelistic outreach, and converts are often better prepared and more likely to bring their own people group to Christ than the missionaries from whom they first received the Gospel. Otte treated the Chinese as a people with a unique culture of their own; they needed the Gospel, not Westernization. This approach undoubtedly increased the ripple effect that extended from the hospitals he established. Otte touched people's bodies by his medical knowledge and provided holistic healing through a ministry of hope and love. Moreover, he trained Chinese Christians to do the kind of ministry that he did for their own people. Thus, the spiritual and physical healing Otte brought to this corner of southeast China continued far beyond his own lifetime and the lifetimes of his patients.

Bibliography

Primary Sources

Collection 318 Papers of Lemuel Nelson Bell. Archives of the Billy Graham Center, Wheaton, IL.

John A. Otte Papers. H88-0117. Joint Archives of Holland, Holland, MI.

Reformed Church in America. *The Seventieth Annual Report of the Board of Foreign Missions of the Reformed Church in America.* New York: Board of Publication of the Reformed Protestant Dutch Church, 1902.

Secondary Sources

De Jong, Gerald F. *The Reformed Church in China, 1842–1951.* Historical Series of the Reformed Church in America 22. Grand Rapids: Eerdmans, 1992.

Pollock, John Charles. *A Foreign Devil in China: The Story of Dr. L. Nelson Bell, an American Surgeon in China.* Minneapolis: World Wide Publications, 1988.

Spence, Jonathan D. *The Search for Modern China.* 3rd ed. New York: Norton, 2013.

---

77. De Jong, *The Reformed Church in China*, 44, quoting Rev. Talmage, an early missionary of the RCA in China and an influence on Dr. Otte.

2

Cultural Exchange
The Story of William Angus and His Poetry

Eric Dawson

WILLIAM ANGUS SERVED AS a missionary for the Reformed Church in America in China's Fujian[1] province from 1925 to 1951.[2] During his time in China, Angus wrote over three hundred poems. When he edited the poems after his return to the United States, he classified them into five separate books. These remained unpublished until 2015,[3] and there is no evidence of their use in research at the time of this writing. Yet, Angus's poetry is a valuable avenue to understanding one missionary's experience, revealing his transition from one culture to another, the efforts this one Westerner made to fit into Chinese culture. The poems not only show how difficult it was for the missionary to cross from one culture to another, but they also reveal the limits of such cultural crossings despite the missionary's best efforts. In Angus's case, his poems confirm how natural it was for missionaries and local Chinese to notice the differences in one another. Moreover,

---

1. Formerly known as Fukien.

2. William Robertson Angus Jr. (1901–84) was born in New York City, graduated from Rutgers University in 1922, Hartford Seminary in 1925, and did graduate work at Yale University.

3. William Angus, *South Fukien: Missionary Poems, 1925–1951*.

these poems demonstrate the delicate nature of Angus's privileged position as an American. The Western missionary's status was, surprisingly, at times manipulated by local Chinese Christians to further their own ends.

Angus's poetry challenges the too often one-sided charge against Western missionaries of forcing their culture on an indigenous people. By incorporating a critical understanding of what has been termed "cultural imperialism," I will show how the convergence of two cultures was more an exchange than an imposition by one side upon the other. China was not a passive recipient of Western culture, for the Chinese environment also affected the missionaries. Finally, I will examine Angus's faith journey, with special emphasis on his spiritual progression as seen in the evolution of his perspectives on material possessions and money.

The Christian mission field in China has a long, troubled history. In his *Disciples of All Nations*, Lamin Sanneh acknowledges that China's early encounters with Christianity in the eighteenth century, a full century before the Protestant missionary movement to China began, was fraught with tension and suspicion. He gives the example of Emperor Yongzheng's Edict of Expulsion and Confiscation, which expelled Catholic missionaries from China and confiscated church property in China. Conscious of the potential impact a foreign religion would have on his country, Yongzheng reversed his predecessor's friendly relations with Jesuit missionaries and persecuted Chinese Christians. In the following century, Yongzheng's fears seemed to be proved right by the First Opium War (1839–42), fought by his successor and Great Britain. The conflict reinforced China's view of Westerners as dangerous. The subsequent unequal treaties opened China to both trade and missionary activity, and extra-territoriality gave Westerners in China—traders and missionaries alike—special legal privileges exempting them from Chinese law. The result was the emergence of strong anti-Western attitudes as Western missionaries entered China to bring the gospel to its people. For much of the nineteenth and twentieth centuries, Christianity in China was associated with Western military encroachment and the foreign culture of the despised Westerners.[4]

This association of Christianity with Western culture was not unique to the missionary movement to China. In fact, Sanneh notes that mission stations in Africa were "imagined little bits of Europe rolled up and transplanted to a foreign country. Their walls contained a European civilization, and outside them were heathen, unenlightened elements of culture.

---

4. Sanneh, *Disciples of All Nations*, 245–46.

Missions represented the boundary delineating one world from another, the age of civilization from the age of heathen customs."[5] This is the predominant contemporary view of the mission field—Western missionaries arriving in foreign locations, bringing along their religion and Western culture. Sanneh argues persuasively that Christianity is distinct from Christendom and Western cultural achievements.

However, even though missionary communities often mirrored this image, William Angus's missionary career offers a counter example to Sanneh's critique of the nineteenth-century missionary movement. His letters, sermons, and especially his poems, give an account of someone who lived among the Chinese people. Even though his life among the Chinese people is an essential story to tell, it does not reflect the typical narrative, a point that Angus himself noted. On December 13, 1943, he wrote to his wife, "I live cheaply out here compared to the others because I have no servants and am on the road practically all the time." He continued, "For three nights I slept on the counter in Gan's shop."[6] Angus's writings show him traveling from town to town, living alongside the local people, with far fewer resources than that commanded by other missionaries. Rather than live as if he were still in the United States, Angus tried to adapt to the conditions in which ordinary Chinese lived in the early twentieth century, thereby illustrating the power and sufficiency of the gospel in all circumstances. In a sermon he delivered in 1969, during his retirement years in the US, Angus recalled his experience in China: "My work in China was done mainly in cooperation with Chinese pastors and preachers, traveling with them, visiting them, talking with them, listening to their stories, stories of themselves, of their lives and work, or stories told to them by others."[7] His ministry was founded upon relationships with local Chinese. Angus was personable and down-to-earth, often conversing with Chinese peasants about crops and soil. He had majored in agricultural science at Rutgers University, and this training served him well in rural China.[8]

---

5. Sanneh, *Disciples of All Nations*, 220.

6. William Angus to Dear Dolly [Mrs. Angus], 13 December 1943, folder "Correspondence, 1942–43," William R. Angus Jr. Papers, H00–1381, Joint Archives of Holland, Holland, MI.

7. William Angus, "World Day of Prayer, February 21, 1969," sermon, folder "Sermons and Prayers, 1968–1970, n.d.," William R. Angus Jr. Papers.

8. David Angus, interview by Marc Baer, Claire Barrett, Katelyn Dickerson, Victoria Longfield, and Gloria Tseng, 21 July 2014, Hope College, Holland, MI.

Angus organized his poetry into five books. The title he gave each book expressed an aspect of his missionary career in China, covering the period from 1925 to 1951 roughly: *Change, Unrest, War, Inflation*, and *Communism*. This chapter draws from all five books to reflect the full range of his experiences, but special emphasis is given to *Change* and *Inflation* in order to examine closely the two themes they explore. *Change* deals principally with Angus's initial reactions to the otherness of China, and *Inflation* presents Angus's observations and opinions on the subject of money. The material for Angus's poems came from his interactions with people. Almost all his poems tell a story. Sometimes Angus was the one who experienced the story firsthand, but often his poems retell stories that he first heard from a Chinese friend or acquaintance. Thus, many poems commence with the words of someone other than Angus. For example, "Measure for Measure" begins with "'I *thought* I wasn't getting enough rice,' said Liau."[9] The poem goes on to tell the story of Liau's frustration. It is evident that Angus spent considerable time with ordinary Chinese, who were the inspiration for his many stories.

Angus's poetry shows that he constantly interacted with local Chinese, which is contrary to the common image, that of missionaries living in a world apart, from this period. Many of Angus's observations in his poems could only have come from proximity to the people whose stories he recounted. The poem "Skeleton" is a moving example. In this poem Angus relates a visit he paid a dying man who had been in charge of writing the weekly bulletin of the church but was now too ill to attend church. The man was an opium addict. Angus told this story in the first person: "I praised his work and told him how glad for the church I was that he gave them his help in difficult matters. I reproached myself for negligent ignorance in omitting to visit a person of such importance."[10] Here we have a picture of a Western missionary entering the home of a Chinese man and the intimate space of one who was facing the end of life. Angus engaged with the local people on their own terms and turf. He did not remain in a world apart.

It is this willingness to enter the world of the local people that gave Angus ample opportunities to encounter "the other," and he reflected on this "otherness" by way of poetry. Angus was the product of a culture

---

9. William Angus, "Measure for Measure," folder "Bound Copies, Blue Carbon – Book Four: Inflation, n.d.," William R. Angus Jr. Papers.

10. William Angus, "Skeleton," folder "Bound Copies, Blue Carbon – Book One: Change, n.d.," William R. Angus Jr. Papers.

very different than that of the people he was meeting on the mission field. Despite his best efforts, Angus could not become one with the Chinese people just by desiring it. He held specific beliefs and ideas because of his American upbringing. Anyone crossing from one culture to another carries preconceptions and cultural expectations, and, naturally, when people of two cultures meet, certain practices of the other culture will seem strange. This strangeness can surface in the most surprising places, and sometimes it is difficult to distinguish between cultural differences and disparity of living standards. The poem "Ah, Insects!" tells about Angus paying a visit to a Chinese man. The host offered the guest some lychees, which the latter was unable to enjoy because of his disgust at discovering worms in every lychee nut.[11] The focal point of the visit became for Angus the worm-infested fruit, and the purpose of the visit seems to have been lost, at least from the poem. His surprise and disgust with the Chinese man's nonchalance toward fruit worms shows the disparity between the living conditions in China and America in the early twentieth century, and the challenges such disparity presented to the missionary feeling his way in a foreign culture.

Not only did Angus perceive the "otherness" of the Chinese, but he was also sensitive enough to realize the strangeness of his own culture in the eyes of the other. An example of this appears in "Mailman's Report," which humorously tells of a Chinese mailman describing Western cultural practices to fellow passengers on a boat. Angus was among the passengers:

> They don't eat rice. They eat wheat bread and cow's milk and butter. They don't use chopsticks like us; they don't know how to use chopsticks. And when they prepare a chicken they cut off the head and throw it away. Then they cut off the feet and throw them away too. The insides, like the intestines, they say are dirty, and so they won't eat them either. The other men's mouths dropped open. They looked at me for confirmation. I nodded. "That's right," I said.[12]

Through the mailman's words the reader can imagine the flourish with which he told his story and perhaps Angus's amusement in observing the scene. To the boatload of Chinese passengers, Western food preparation practices must have seemed unimaginably wasteful. It is unsurprising that one's observations of the other often involve food, which has the power

11. William Angus, "Ah! Insects!" folder "Bound Copies, Blue Carbon – Book One: Change, n.d."

12. William Angus, "Mailman's Report," folder "Bound Copies, Blue Carbon – Book One: Change, n.d."

to elicit curiosity, pleasure, and disgust, and is often the first ingredient of relationships. Here one observes Angus coming to see his own culture from a Chinese man's perspective, whereas in "Ah! Insects!" one sees a Western guest's "gut reaction" to wormy fruit offered by his Chinese host.

As earnestly as Angus wanted to be one among the Chinese people, he could not escape the "otherness" of his Western appearance. He rarely focused on himself in his poems, but the few times he did, he expressed frustration with his Western identity and physical appearance. For example, in "Blue Monday," Angus wrote, "Where is my witness? I went out in the street: 'Go-wah! Here is a man as big as two or three men.' I witnessed to the hugeness of Americans."[13] While humorous, it nevertheless displayed his irritation with being much bigger than every Chinese. Standing six feet, two inches tall, when Angus was out in the sun his face turned quite red, and he was known among local Christians as Pastor Ang, or Pastor "Red" in the local dialect. He was clearly conspicuous in the Chinese villages he visited.[14] In this case, physical appearance marked Angus as distinctly other, however hard he tried to be one among the Chinese.

In addition to culture and physical appearance, Western missionaries were also "other" in their economically privileged position in China. Even though going to the mission field entailed real material sacrifices on the part of the men and women who answered God's call, missionaries nonetheless enjoyed a much higher standard of living than their Chinese neighbors. In "I Say Nothing," Angus reflected on his position as compared with the local Chinese. After acknowledging that his salary was ten times that of ordinary Chinese, he carried on a debate with himself: "Share my own salary? I have a wife and three children; my house was looted, my savings lost in Shanghai; we answer many smaller calls for help, and I'm in debt now. I wish I could live more cheaply, but I don't know how to make such a big adjustment."[15] The poem shows Angus's conflicting feelings about his economic position. In effect, Angus was confined by the privileged lifestyle he enjoyed in China. He wanted to be one among the Chinese people, but he was unwilling or unable to share fully in their material privations.

---

13. William Angus, "Blue Monday," folder "Bound Copies, Blue Carbon – Book Two: Unrest, n.d.," William R. Angus Jr. Papers.

14. David Angus, interview.

15. William Angus, "I Say Nothing," folder "Bound Copies, Blue Carbon – Book Two: Unrest, n.d."

Angus evidenced much sensitivity in his attitude toward material possessions. In 1932, bandits looted his house. Much of his identity was intertwined with his American lifestyle. Although he was not rich, he nevertheless had far more than most Chinese, and he held tightly to certain possessions. The robbery led him to search his own heart:

> III
> Money we spent for things,
> Bright rugs and curtains,
> Linens and finer stuffs,
> Crystal and silver.
>
> Books without end I bought,
> Fondled the bindings,
> Ranged them upon my shelves,
> Packed and unpacked them,
>
> Read them and looked at them,
> Babbled about them all;
> No one need read a book
> When I had finished.
>
> IV
> Ay, where the treasure is
> There is the heart too.
> And I have thought of it,
> Scolded my folly.
> "Yes, Lord," I often said,
> "If these things hinder,
> Teach me to let them go
> Or take them from me."[16]

Angus was attached to his books, carpets, linens and so on, and the loss of these things shook him to the core. Who would fault him for it? Yet, he saw in the robbery an opportunity for soul searching and spiritual growth:

> VI
> What if He come like flame
> Making me stranger to

---

16. William Angus, "After the Looting," folder "Bound Copies, Blue Carbon – Book Two: Unrest, n.d."

All the sweet lusts of life? . . .
Still I must ask it."[17]

Indeed, this was radical obedience to the call to love not the world!

Scholars such as Sanneh have critiqued missionaries for their inappropriate use of power. However, either missionaries were not always conscious of the extent of their power, or, try as they might, they could not escape the reality of their privileged status. "Occupied Chapel" tells of the takeover of a local church by some rebels. After talking with Angus, the rebel leader agreed to leave the church peacefully in six weeks. Angus considered this a victory, but when he reported it back to the Chinese preacher, the preacher was upset:

> I reported our visit to the preacher.
> He was disappointed. He complained, "You were too easy.
> Six weeks! He'll not get out of that place in six weeks.
> He's planning to run his school for a whole year there.
> No room! He has plenty of places to put his men in.
> You should have asked him to go, let him take it or leave it.
> We can't talk to him that way, but you're an American
> And can use your foreign prestige to tell him things."
>
> I felt the self-esteem hiss out of me.
> "Suppose I said to get out and he didn't do it?"
>
> "All right, you should have said it and let him choose.
> If he didn't get out, you could take it up in Changchow,[18]
> Or with your consul."
>
> "No," I said, "I couldn't.
> I didn't go to see that man as an American;
> I went there as moderator of the Soa '-sia' Church,
> Appointed by our classis, else I wouldn't have gone.
> And if I complain to the army, it's with the committee
> Appointed by Synod and representing the church."
>
> "That's what *you* say," he grumbled, "not what *he thinks*.

---

17. William Angus, "After the Looting."

18. Spelled Zhangzhou in modern pinyin, Changchow was one of the up-country stations of the Amoy Mission; Soa-sia was one of the churches under its supervision.

He wouldn't listen to you if you weren't a foreigner."[19]

In both the eyes of the rebel leader and the Chinese preacher, Angus had special power because he had the American consul behind him. Angus may have seen himself as someone who served under the classis and was appointed by the synod, both under indigenous leadership; yet, all this respect for indigenous leadership did not matter, for it was the privileged status of Angus as a Westerner protected by the might of his home country that mattered. Angus could not escape the fact that Westerners were in a league of their own.

There were other incidents in which Angus's status as a Westerner was exploited. "Ignorance" tells of a Chinese woman who ran away from her husband, a local pastor. When she was found, she cleverly asked Angus to take her back to her husband's home. A Chinese church member informed Angus of her real intentions: "Well, now, you see, you promise to take her back home to the pastor's house. Then you're responsible! She goes along with you but never gets there, runs off with this other fellow. The father knows nothing – the other family'll never ask *you* to pay because you don't know our customs."[20] Because of his Western status, Chinese law and customs did not apply to Angus. It was not only missionaries who took advantage of their own legal privileges, but the Chinese who were in the missionaries' sphere of influence also tried to exploit these privileges when an occasion arose. In this case, Angus almost became an accomplice in a Chinese woman's attempt to escape from an unhappy marriage.

Cultural stereotyping forms an important element in the common understanding of missionaries from the West. Historian Ryan Dunch explores the validity and meaning behind what is termed "cultural imperialism." He examines the postcolonial critique of Westerners imposing their culture on indigenous cultures. More specifically, in the religious realm he observes that missionaries "are routinely portrayed in both literature and scholarship as narrow-minded chauvinists whose presence and preaching destroyed indigenous cultures and opened the way for the extension of colonial rule."[21] He argues, however, that when two cultures come into contact, cultural influences flow both ways, and one does not simply dominate the other. Dunch

---

19. William Angus, "Occupied Chapel," folder "Bound Copies, Blue Carbon – Book Two: Unrest, n.d."

20. William Angus, "Ignorance," folder "Bound Copies, Blue Carbon – Book One: Change, n.d."

21. Dunch, "Beyond Cultural Imperialism," 307.

states that cultures are not "solid objects that collide like billiard balls, displacing one in favor of another."[22] Cultures are fluid, and the receptors of a new culture are as influential and responsible as the transmitters, and even in situations of unequal power, the less powerful party still has agency.

Angus's stories illustrate Dunch's argument well. In "Occupied Chapel," the preacher says to Angus with indignation, "You should have asked him to go, let him take it or leave it. / *We* can't talk to him that way, but you're an American / And can use your foreign prestige to tell him things."[23] Angus may have wanted to avoid appearing as the "Western imperialist," but the Chinese preacher simply wanted to get the rebels to leave his chapel as soon as possible, and he saw nothing wrong in taking advantage of Angus's American influence to achieve this end. In fact, he believed that Angus *should have* used it to that end. Angus was aware of how things looked from the perspective of the Chinese Christians, as his poem "Cases" shows: "You see our position. We stood for the powerful West, / For influence in the right place. If we wouldn't *use* it, / Our Chinese friends often felt that we had betrayed them."[24] Local Chinese Christians expected Angus to help them by using his political power. However, Angus was conscious of the impact this had on the church, noting that "these cases roused hatred against the Church."[25] Missionaries were not the only ones responsible for taking advantage of foreign political power. As the above two poems illustrate, Chinese Christians encouraged Angus to use his privilege for their benefit. In fact, Angus was very much aware of his special position as a Westerner in China and how tempting it was for Chinese Christians to want to use it in disputes with fellow Chinese. He resisted pressures from Chinese Christians to do so, even when it caused tension between him and his Chinese Christian friends. The poem "Bad Shepherds" describes the reaction of Chinese Christians when Angus refused a request by Chinese Christians to take a case to court on their behalf: "They turned to me. / But I sat there in silence until they gave up, / Dismissing me as a self-willed foreigner."[26] Angus incurred the displeasure of Chinese Christians who came to him

---

22. Dunch, "Beyond Cultural Imperialism," 312.

23. Angus, "Occupied Chapel."

24. William Angus, "Cases," folder "Bound Copies, Blue Carbon – Book One: Change, n.d."

25. William Angus, "Cases."

26. William Angus, "Bad Shepherds," folder "Bound Copies, Blue Carbon – Book One: Change, n.d."

for help because he was unwilling to use his privileged status the way they wanted him to. He withheld his power because he did not believe it was appropriate to use it in that way. The relationship between missionaries and Chinese became quite complex, and was, in effect, a two-way street. Angus's poems show how local Chinese Christians tugged on his political strings to further their own ends, and, more importantly, how Angus often refused to be manipulated because he realized the negative effect the use of Western privilege had on the Chinese church.

Chinese Christians were not the only ones who tried to take advantage of Angus because he was a Westerner. In fact, people who did not know Angus personally tried to do that as well, mainly for financial gain. The poem "Wounds" tells the story of some Chinese soldiers who tried to swindle Angus. One of the soldiers, dressed up as an injured villager, had two other soldiers bring him to Angus. They claimed that they had rescued the "injured villager" from bandits and wanted a reward. However, Angus saw through what the soldiers were doing and called their bluff: "Hmm, this is pretty bad; I'll have to take him upstairs and cut him right open."[27] After hearing this, the impostor "came to with a snap."[28] Humorous as the incident was, its backdrop was the unsavory reality of Western privilege in China, and the wealth associated with such privilege. Whether he wanted to or not, Angus shared in its benefits. The soldiers assumed Angus to be wealthy, for he was a Westerner, and they expected him to reward "a good deed" perhaps because he was a missionary. They were opportunists attempting to profit from a situation of inequality, and Angus, to his credit, did not fall for the trap.

The issue of foreign power and privilege was more often a source of rancor than of humor, however. In the poem "A Free Hand" the narrator tells the reader that it was very hard for the church to get any members in his area, except for children of Christians and people who had come from elsewhere. There was deep-seated antagonism to the church: "Years ago, in all the clan houses, / The big clans posted notices, putting a curse / On any person who became a Christian."[29] This hostility originated in the

---

27. William Angus, "Wounds," folder "Bound Copies, Blue Carbon – Book One: Change, n.d."

28. William Angus, "Wounds."

29. William Angus, "A Free Hand," folder "Bound Copies, Blue Carbon – Book One: Change, n.d."

aftermath of the infamous Boxer Rebellion,[30] decades prior to the setting of the poem. A man from another church was passing through the region and was robbed by bandits. He went to see the preacher, and the two went to see the local magistrate. The magistrate collected a huge sum of fines on behalf of the victim of the robbery and the preacher:

> ... The official, proclaiming the threat
> Of foreign intervention on their behalf
> As persecuted Christians, collected in fines
> Over a hundred thousand dollars.[31] Of this,
> He gave the Christian about four thousand, more
> Than he'd lost in the first place. That is what gave him his start.
> And he is a rich man now. But the church has suffered.[32]

In this story, Christianity, backed by "foreign intervention," was used as an opportunity to make money. The Christian victim benefited, and the magistrate benefited even more, pocketing what he did not give the man. It is no wonder that Christianity and foreign control were understood as being intimately connected. The stereotype of Western imperialism was not unfounded.

"Answer" is Angus's most revealing poem on the delicate issue of Western missionaries using their special status on behalf of the church. It is worth considering in its entirety to recapture the complexities of personalities from two cultures traversing the two-way street:

> The pastor and preacher, both young fellows, came to see me.
> "The soldiers are in the Sin-tng Chapel," they said,
> "And act as if they intend to stay there. The work
> We planned for the fall will be upset by this.
> We wondered if you would go with us to headquarters

---

30. An anti-foreign peasant rebellion that began in north China in 1898 and culminated in the summer of 1900, when a foreign expeditionary force of about 20,000 men defeated the Boxer rebels. About 250 foreigners, most of whom were missionaries, and roughly 30,000 Chinese Christians were killed by Boxers; China was made to pay a huge indemnity of 450 million taels (around $333 million at the then current exchange rates) for the loss of foreign lives and damages to foreign property. See Spence, *The Search for Modern China*, 2nd edition, 230–33; Bays, *A New History of Christianity in China*, 85–86.

31. It is not clear from the poem what the actual currency unit was. It was most likely not US dollars. Given that it was the beginning of the twentieth century, it could have been the Chinese currency unit *qian* or the Mexican silver dollar.

32. William Angus, "A Free Hand."

And ask them to order the soldiers to move. Nanking[33]
Has sent out orders protecting Christian churches."

"But you have Synod's committee to handle these things,"
I said, "and the chairman's here. Let *him* go with you."

"But you're an American. They'll listen to *you*."

"*You* listen to me," I said. "You're both young men.
You know all this talk of foreign imperialism.
You hate it and so do I. In earlier days
The Christians were always running to the consul
To see that they got their rights, and now our religion's
Called foreign. They've got us tied up to consuls and courts,
Running dogs of imperialism, enslaving China."

"We aren't talking about the consul," they said.
"We just want you to help us out here at headquarters.
You've been there to help out Soa '-sia' several times."

"That's right. I went there to help the Soa '-sia' Church.
But I was their moderator, appointed by Classis.
I went as a representative of the Church,
Not as an American. That didn't make any difference,
I was an American anyhow. I know.
I've heard that before, and it's true, but it's not why I went.
I had status. I won't go with you. I have no status."

"That makes no difference."

"No? Well, it does to me.
The pastor and the committee chairman should go.
But if you think I'm wrong," I said at last,
"I'll go next door and ask my colleague about it."

They grinned resignedly. "We've been there already.
He says the same thing you say."

I grinned too.[34]

33. Nanjing in modern pinyin. From 1928 to 1937, the outbreak of the Second Sino-Japanese War, Nanjing was the capital of China under the Nationalist government.

34. William Angus, "Answer," folder "Bound Copies, Blue Carbon – Book Two: Unrest, n.d."

This dialogue illustrates Chinese Christians attempting to use Angus's privileged status as a Westerner for the church's benefit, and the length to which Angus went to resist their pressure. The end of the poem suggests that the young men knew Angus would say no and perhaps even respected him for it. The dialogue also reveals the existence of Angus's colleague, who was of the same mind that the church should not rely on Western power. Yet, this scene reveals the delicate nature of the issue. In historical hindsight, Chinese Christians' reliance on Western might and prestige could not be anything but detrimental to the Chinese church and the prospects of the advancement of the gospel in China. But in the historical moment, in a lawless situation where might meant right, one could very well sympathize with the Chinese Christians' desire to fall back on the one expediency at their disposal. What mattered to them was getting soldiers or bandits—the line between the two was often blurred—out of their property. Was it so wrong to use Western influence to protect the church? Were not the missionaries who refused to "help" being unnecessarily obstinate?

In addition to physical appearance, the Westerner's privileged status, and culinary habits, Chinese attitudes toward women were another area in which Angus observed the "otherness" of the Chinese people, or his own "otherness" in the eyes of the Chinese. Angus wrote many poems on the Chinese view of women. In that era, it was common for daughters to be given away or sold in times of distress, or even killed at birth in extreme circumstances, for they were seen as a drain on a family's scarce resources. In the poem "Monkey-Demon," a Chinese Christian family decides to keep a daughter with a birth defect. The father states, "The neighbors said to me, you certainly were a Christian to keep that child, for none of us would ever have bothered with her. It's true, they'd have killed her all right, a girl like that."[35] In a cultural context where even healthy baby girls were merely tolerated, to keep a baby girl with a birth defect was certainly extraordinary. The poem bears testimony to this sad fact of life in early twentieth-century China and to a profound change in values brought about by Christianity. The standing of women in Chinese society is one of the recurrent themes in Angus's poetry. The poem "Offer" tells the story of a poor geese seller who tried to sell her daughter to Angus instead of the geese.[36] This shocked

---

35. William Angus, "Monkey-Demon," folder "Bound Copies, Blue Carbon – Book One: Change, n.d."

36. William Angus, "Offer," folder "Bound Copies, Blue Carbon – Book Three: War, n.d.," William R. Angus Jr. Papers.

Angus, but, then, his experiences in China continued to show him that the Chinese people viewed women much differently than he and his fellow missionaries did.

Sometimes Angus responded with wry humor to what he heard people say. The poem "Another Advantage" retells a conversation about food prices in which Angus took part:

> As we were eating, someone happened to say,
> "Rice is so high across the Kwangtung[37] border
> They're selling off their women for almost nothing.
> You can get a wife down there for the price of two geese."
> "Why," I said, "you could carry four geese down
> And carry two wives back."
> "That's not necessary,"
> Said one of the younger men, "the women could walk."
> The others gravely assured me that this was so.[38]

This poem is a poignant reflection of both the economic privation and the social attitudes of the time. The high price of rice, a staple, to the point that it was worth more than a human being, evidenced the hardship experienced by ordinary people in early twentieth-century China. That a woman could be had for the price of two geese reflected the attitude that women were mere property, and not very valuable property, one might add. Without hearing Angus's tone of voice, one is not quite sure what to make of his quip: "Why, you could carry four geese down and carry two wives back." Was he being ironic? If he was, those who assured him matter-of-factly that women could walk and did not need to be carried certainly missed his irony. Could he have become so inured to the harsh conditions surrounding him daily that he was simply bantering with these men, or, was this an understated commentary on the poor treatment of women in China in this era? Compared to his sympathetic treatment of Chinese women in some of his other poems, "Another Advantage" is rather ambiguous, but it nonetheless shows Angus engaging with the economic and social realities around him and in turn being shaped or affected by them in some way.

---

37. Guangdong in modern pinyin.

38. William Angus, "Another Advantage," folder "Bound Copies, Blue Carbon – Book Three: War, n.d."

Angus's engagement with the socio-economic realities of the ordinary Chinese among whom he lived was especially evident in his wrestling with the issue of money. When he first arrived in China, Angus saw money as a potential solution for some of China's social problems. "My Blunder," which appears among his earlier poems in his first book of poetry, tells of an incident in which a local Chinese man asked Angus for aid for two of his students. Without much thought, Angus offered the man money. But the Chinese man felt insulted by Angus's response because he was looking for hospitality, not money.[39] Angus's naive reaction of parting with the money instead of giving his time revealed that he had entered China believing that money could solve some of China's social issues. However, after spending several decades in China, he came to an understanding that money, in fact, interfered with the opportunity to deepen relationships.

In his fourth book of poetry, *Inflation*, Angus discussed money in nearly every poem. In these compositions, it is clear that money and Angus's faith journey were intimately connected. In "What Price Rescue?" Angus observed the value that the Chinese people placed on money. The poem describes a haunting scene in which a boat capsized near a port: "And many small boats put out to rescue the people, / but not indiscriminately. They bargained with them; / how much will you give me if I save you? Some / agreed to anything and climbed into the boat; / others backed off and looked for another rescuer. / And others gave up and drowned; the price was too high."[40] Drowning people were denied rescue because they could not afford to pay. The poem does not explicitly say that this is wrong or unjust, but other poems reveal Angus's frustration with money, making the missionary's vague stance in this poem clearer. For example, "Profit for God" tells the story, in the first person, of a man who came from a very rich family that was ripped apart by strife: "There was my father, and there were five of us brothers, / All dissolute, headstrong, quarrelsome. Always fighting. / Almost every night we drank and gambled and fought. / My father would get drunk and scream at my brothers / and they would fight with him until the servants / Pulled them away and helped them to their rooms."[41] The man eventually heard the gospel after running away to join

39. William Angus, "My Blunder," folder "Bound Copies, Blue Carbon – Book One: Change, n.d."

40. William Angus, "What Price Rescue?" folder "Bound Copies, Blue Carbon – Book Four: Inflation, n.d."

41. William Angus, "Profit for God," folder "Bound Copies, Blue Carbon – Book Four: Inflation, n.d."

the army. After that, he evangelized wherever the Spirit led him; preaching was his newfound purpose in life: "I have no thought / If the place to which I am led is large or small, / The people few or many, rich or poor. / I want to do what God would have me do / And my endeavor in every situation / Is to make a profit for God."[42] The man was now more interested in his relationship with God and others than in money. That Angus wrote about this suggests that he was inspired by the dramatic transformation of this man's life, his shift from loving money to loving God. The poem highlights this change in its conclusion, which describes the man's reaction to being short-changed in a financial transaction: "And I could have argued the point. I was bigger than he was / And I wasn't afraid of him. But I thought to myself, / 'If you start a row, you may get the right price for your ring, / And that will be profit, but will it be profit for God?'"[43] The man described in "Profit for God" contrasts sharply with the "rescuers" described in "What Price Rescue?" In these poems, the reader sees Angus pondering the effects that the love of money has on the human heart. Might Angus have been examining his own heart as he wrote these poems? He might well have had these words of Jesus in mind as he reflected on the people he was writing about: "No one can serve two masters, for either he will hate the one and love the other, or he will be devoted to the one and despise the other. You cannot love God and money."[44]

Even when it was given for a good cause such as humanitarian relief, money could have undesirable effects that were unforeseen. "Post-War Relief" speaks, in the voice of a Chinese, of the relief aid sent from America to the people of Xiamen after the end of the Second World War: "down here in Amoy we'd be better off if we never saw any relief. It rouses the worst in everyone, greed, dishonesty, jealousy."[45] Although Angus did not overtly claim that money caused "greed, dishonesty, and jealousy," his writing of these poems nevertheless shows that he was aware of money's potential for both doing good and arousing the worst in the human heart. For the sake of money, the people in the story of the capsized boat willingly allowed others to drown, whereas the people in the story told in "Post-War Relief" showed remarkable awareness of the harm caused by the desire for money.

42. William Angus, "Profit for God."
43. William Angus, "Profit for God."
44. Matt 6:24 (ESV).
45. William Angus, "Post-War Relief," folder "Bound Copies, Blue Carbon – Book Four: Inflation, n.d."

Angus's poems not only illustrate the effects of China's dismal economy in the first half of the twentieth century, but they also show Angus questioning the role of money. Perhaps he asked himself, Was money the answer to China's struggles? Could a regeneration of the hearts of her people also be necessary even as their material needs had to be met?

Callous "rescuers" at the scene of a capsized boat and greedy recipients of relief aid from America, presumably nonbelievers, were not the only people who could be ensnared by the love of money. A long narrative poem of some one hundred twenty lines, "A Moneyed Man," tells the sad story of a gifted Chinese preacher named Iau, with whom Angus worked for years, from Angus's first-person voice in response to a certain Bill's inquiry concerning Iau's request for a raise that was rejected by the Preachers' Central Committee:

> He got the full schedule and the allowances
> For men in special work. I don't claim it's enough;
> It's merely what the rest get. I could use
> My own money to supplement his income, but that
> Is neither wise nor necessary. He's a rich man.
> He's about the only preacher we have
> Who's entirely independent financially,
> But he's always in some squabble over salary.
> He's a wonderful speaker; I hate to see him retire
> But that's his own choice, not mine. He wants extra money
> Not because of need, but because of prestige,
> Because he thinks he's worth it, and he is.[46]

Iau "was the best evangelist we had, / And one of the finest speakers I've ever heard."[47] His father had left him an income of "between two and three tons of unhulled rice a year,"[48] which *should have* given him the freedom to preach the gospel without financial worry. He knew the Bible well and was well-versed in the Chinese classics. He could hold an audience of believers and nonbelievers alike spellbound with his preaching. Yet, his ministry—first as a traveling evangelist and then as a pastor of a local Chinese church—was marked by yearly squabbles over salary and ended prematurely when

---

46. William Angus, "A Moneyed Man," folder "Bound Copies, Blue Carbon – Book Four: Inflation, n.d."
47. William Angus, "A Moneyed Man."
48. William Angus, "A Moneyed Man."

he so alienated the church he pastored that the consistory called another pastor. It is a sad tale of the stunted spiritual life of a minister of the gospel who had started out with great potential. One can almost hear the regret over such a life in Angus's voice:

> So Iau, fifty-two, retired. He played well the role
> Of retired preacher, referred to himself as old
> And decrepit, reminisced brilliantly on occasion,
> Told of the brilliant career of his eldest son,
> Made witty welcome addresses and masterful speeches
> At anniversaries, conferences, and so forth,
> And took good care of his property and investments.[49]

Angus was a keen observer of people, and even his observations of outrageous events or deeply flawed people were narrated with great sensitivity. His gaze was directed not only at those around him but also at himself. It is fitting to recall at this point his poem "After the Looting," in which he lay before God his own attachment to his prized possessions following a robbery. In his poems, one gets a glimpse into not only the political, social, and economic conditions of early twentieth-century China but also the spiritual journey of a lifelong missionary.

In all, William Angus committed close to thirty years of his life to missionary work in China. Many of his experiences were recorded in the numerous poems that he wrote over the course of those three decades. In them, the reader sees the interactions between a Western missionary and the ordinary Chinese among whom he lived. In light of the scholarship on missionaries, his experiences add complexity to the typical story of missionaries in early twentieth-century China. Western imperialism was a geopolitical reality in which Angus, his fellow missionaries, and the Chinese people lived in the early twentieth century. Angus was deeply aware of the burden that it placed on the Chinese church, but it was very tempting for Chinese Christians to want to fall back on a Westerner's privileged position in China when they wanted quick redress for a wrong in a lawless situation. Moreover, China was not only a "target" of evangelization for Angus, but this "mission field" was also the field in which Angus the missionary was formed spiritually over a lifetime. As his poems show, when two cultures come together, one does not necessarily override the other. Instead, the two cultures may be in conflict, or engage in an exchange. Because of

---

49. William Angus, "A Moneyed Man."

this exchange, the relationship between the missionary and the indigenous people is usually complex. In looking at the relationship between the two cultures—Chinese and American—it is vital to note that each party brought something to the table. Often, certain dishes on a dinner table may appear more prominent than others. In any case, one must not lose sight of the rest of the meal just because the main dish is in front and at the center of the table. Angus's radical example of living simply among ordinary Chinese is a fitting illustration of the sufficiency and power of the gospel, which, in Lamin Sanneh's understanding, "had its religious roots in the deeds and actions of a redemptive God whose claim on faith and obedience was absolute and nonnegotiable."[50] The seed that was sown by the men and women who, like Angus, were willing to step outside the trappings of European civilization is now bearing fruit in the Christian revival of post-Mao China as Chinese Christians work out the implications of the gospel in their own cultural, societal, and national context.[51]

Bibliography

Primary Sources

Angus, David. Interview. July 21, 2014.
William R. Angus Jr. Papers. H00–1381. Joint Archives of Holland, Holland, MI.

Secondary Sources

Bays, Daniel H. *A New History of Christianity in China*. Malden, MA: Wiley-Blackwell, 2012.
Dunch, Ryan. "Beyond Cultural Imperialism: Cultural Theory, Christian Missions, and Global Modernity." *History and Theory* 41/3 (2002) 301–25.
Sanneh, Lamin O. *Disciples of All Nations: Pillars of World Christianity*. New York: Oxford University Press, 2008.
Spence, Jonathan D. *The Search for Modern China*. 2nd ed. New York: Norton, 1999.

---

50. Sanneh, *Disciples of All Nations*, 237.

51. Sanneh, *Disciples of All Nations*, chapter 8 "Christian Awakening and the New China" examines this revival and considers its prospects.

3

THE DUAL CALLING OF MISSIONARY WIVES

Married Women Missionaries of the RCA in China, 1917-1951

VICTORIA LONGFIELD

THIS CHAPTER TELLS NOT only the stories of three remarkable married women of faith but also echoes of others whose stories are lost and not recorded. Stella Veenschoten, Joyce Angus, and Ruth Holleman were women who vibrantly lived out their roles as wives and missionaries in China. Their lives are an inspiration for many who seek to live out the Christian call to serve the Lord in all aspects of their lives. My interest in the roles of missionary wives in China began during my research on missionaries of the Reformed Church in America in the Joint Archives of Holland, Michigan. Much to my chagrin, not many collections are specifically dedicated to the wives, and the few entries that exist are often listed with their husbands' names on the labels of the collections. Earnestly looking into the lives of the few that had their names on collections, I was surprised to find nothing on their actual service in China. As I began to study other collections, I gradually found material with wives listed under their husbands' names. Then I discovered more material that indicated the need for missionary wives in

China as Gospel witnesses. This information and research on the culture of China shaped my understanding of the accomplishments of a missionary wife and her place in China.

Searching for more, I dug deeper into the H. M. Veenschoten Collection and found over 200 letters written by H. M. Veenschoten's wife, Stella, to her parents back in Holland, Michigan, about her life in China. The letters were a great find, and they provided insight into not only Stella's role as a missionary wife but also the roles of other missionary wives who were her friends and contemporaries. Towards the end of my research, I was pleasantly surprised to receive by email a letter written by Joann Hill, daughter of Stella Veenschoten and a former missionary to China herself. How amazing that the now 91-year-old daughter of the missionary about whom I was reading in the archives would write to tell me about her mother and her own experiences as a missionary wife in China! In the email correspondence sent to me and to our mutual acquaintance, Mrs. Hill wrote, "Wonders of electronics never cease to amaze me!"[1] Technology is amazing in its ability to span the country and the world to offer insights to a researcher and to give greater meaning to a project. The stories of these women and their hitherto muted voices can now be heard. The work of these missionary wives and the way they lived out the Gospel call to "make disciples of *all* nations" is inspiring, and the women in this chapter invite readers to answer this call in their own ways.

The Call of the Gospel, a Call to Missionary Work

> Therefore go and make disciples of all nations, baptizing them in the name of the Father and of the Son and of the Holy Spirit, and teaching them to obey everything I have commanded you. And surely I am with you always, to the very end of the age.[2]

People often quote and preach from this Gospel passage as a call to missionary work. Missionary wives were, just like their missionary husbands, strong and faithful Christians who took seriously all aspects of their vocation as missionaries to China. David Angus, son of missionaries to China William and Joyce Angus, would remark many years later,

---

1. Joann Hill, email message to author, June 28, 2014.
2. Matt 28:19–20 (NIV).

"The silent strength was the women."³ These missionary wives were the power behind the men, and their role was vital for the spread of the Gospel throughout China. Although often their role as wives and mothers did not allow for work on the "front lines" of the mission field, the responsibilities they fulfilled as missionaries in China and in caring for their families were significant and influential in the spread of the Gospel. Yet, the two roles that missionary wives played—in the family and in the mission field—were often in tension. Homemaker, mother, and teacher of young children were vital roles to the well-being of the missionary family; evangelism, teaching, and involvement in mission churches were typical roles of the missionary. Missionary wives assumed all these roles, but domestic responsibilities were often imperative and more pressing. Missionary wives made homemaking and meeting the needs of their children their first priority. As the needs of the family decreased over time with children growing older and leaving the home for higher education, the missionary wives gradually took on more roles outside the home and in the mission field.

Unfortunately, very little scholarship exists on the work missionary wives undertook as "missionaries" rather than as "wives." However, it is clear from the sources that discuss the roles of male missionaries that their wives also contributed to the cause. For example, the patriarchal society and culture of China did not allow men to interact with, influence, or convert women in a face-to-face manner.⁴ There had to be a mediator that could take the Gospel to Chinese women. This role was assumed by either male family members of Chinese women or female missionaries in the field. Single women missionaries contributed in two ways: through health care or education. Missionary wives often did not perform these "professional" tasks; nonetheless, they used their skills and abilities in their own work for the Kingdom. The limited availability of relevant primary sources explains the paucity of scholarship on missionary wives.

The role of missionary wives changed greatly during this period. At the beginning of the period discussed in this chapter, the Board of Foreign Missions of the Reformed Church in America (RCA) considered missionary wives "associate missionaries," but at some point between 1917 and 1947, married women were given full missionary status on the field.⁵ How-

---

3. David Angus, interview by Marc Baer, Claire Barrett, Katelyn Dickerson, Victoria Longfield, and Gloria Tseng, 21 July 2014, Hope College, Holland, MI.

4. Hunter, *The Gospel of Gentility*, 90–127.

5. Joann Hill, email message to author, July 8, 2014.

ever, although married women of the RCA were recorded in the annual reports of its Board of Foreign Missions as participating in the work of the Kingdom, accounts of their actual work in the field were few.[6] Likewise, only a few secondary sources discuss the work of missionary wives in the field. For instance, in *The Gospel of Gentility* Jane Hunter argues that the role of the missionary wife was important; yet the need to have her husband's work and her family come first often overshadowed her contribution in the field. Hunter writes,

> Missionary women had not anticipated the vast array of forces that would interfere with their plans for work, nor did they for the most part ever confront those forces. Rather, they experienced their problems as punishments for personal failings.
>
> Women who aspired to Christian service within an expanded women's sphere, which included such areas of public life as schools, hospitals, and churches, found the isolation of their child-rearing years after their husbands' work had begun particularly difficult.[7]

Hunter argues that the needs of the family often hindered what these women really wanted to do, which was to work with Chinese in the field. However, their role in the family was equally important and part of the call of a missionary wife. In a chapter entitled "Conflict and Consensus in Mission Institutions" in his *The British Missionary Enterprise since 1700*, Jeffrey Cox notes that missionary wives had a unique calling and were able to live it out in the mission field despite children and their role as homemakers. For instance, education was a significant part of a missionary wife's work early on in mission history. According to Cox, "Education had been central to the building of Christian institutions since the first days of the missionary movement in the eighteenth century, and missionary wives began schools for girls as part of their natural and normal role as a missionary wife."[8] Both Hunter and Cox agree that by playing two roles in the field, that of

---

6. These annual reports to the denomination's General Synod summarized the work of each mission field of the denomination under several categories: evangelical, educational, and medical. However, the work of married women (although believed to fall under these categories) was not specifically mentioned, whereas men's work was, as well as single women's. The Yale Divinity School Library has a digitized collection of these annual reports—Yale University Library, Divinity Library, Day Missions Collection: Annual Reports, https://web.library.yale.edu/divinity/day-missions-collection-annual-reports-listing (accessed 20 June 2019).

7. Jane Hunter, *The Gospel of Gentility*, 117.

8. Jeffrey Cox, *The British Missionary Enterprise since 1700*, 201.

the homemaker and that of the missionary, missionary wives brought the Gospel to the people of foreign lands.

The work of missionary wives was powerful because it spread the Gospel to people whom their husbands could not reach. Their stories can be pieced together from personal documents. For instance, Stella Veenschoten wrote letters back home to her parents, and that correspondence gave her a lasting voice. These personal sources detail the challenges women faced as wives, mothers, and missionaries in a foreign country. Two roles emerged—one operating in the household and the other in "China"—and evident tension existed between the two in the voices of missionary wives like Stella. Married women had the difficult task of balancing their home life and the call to serve the country of China. However, missionary wives were able to resolve the tension eventually by serving both China and their families over time, slowly shifting their focus from their families to China. The missionary wives of the RCA went overseas with their husbands to the denomination's mission located in Xiamen, China.[9] Many families played different roles in the mission and ministered to the Chinese people in various ways by using their talents in fulfilling their call from God. Although there were about as many missionary wives as there were male missionaries, for most of them were married men, three women's voices in particular have been preserved through personal papers and serve as examples of the dual roles that married women filled in China. Stella Veenschoten (in China 1917–1951), Joyce Angus (1925–1951), and Ruth Holleman (1917–1951) represented different aspects of the roles of the homemaker and missionary to China that married women played.

Stella Girard Veenschoten was born on March 14, 1892, in Pigeon, Michigan.[10] Her father worked for the Pere Marquette Railroad, which brought his family to Holland, Michigan, during Stella's high school years.

---

9. Formerly, the island city of Xiamen was known to the missionaries as Amoy. It is in the southeastern province of Fujian, formerly known as Fukien. The name of the RCA's mission in China was the Amoy Mission.

10. Tena Holkeboer, "Mrs. H. M. Veenschoten," *The Church Herald*, 7 September 1962. Although it is the convention for historians to refer to historical figures by their last names, I intentionally refer to Stella Girard Veenschoten by her first name in this chapter. This decision is for two reasons. First, with her last name changing from Girard to Veenschoten when she married Henry "Nelson" Veenschoten, it is complicated and confusing to refer to her by her last name as Nelson bears the same last name. Second and more importantly, the rationale for this chapter is partially to rectify the lack of recognition for missionary wives, who were usually barely acknowledged for their work and were hardly ever referred to by their first names.

In Holland, while she was playing the piano and singing in the Methodist Church choir, Stella met Henry M. Veenschoten, a student attending Western Theological Seminary who was known as "Nelson."[11] Nelson and Stella were married shortly after Nelson's graduation from seminary in 1917.[12] That same year, they moved to China to become missionaries of the RCA. After studying the Xiamen dialect, the Veenschotens moved to Zhangzhou[13] to take up their post as missionary evangelists. Stella steadily became more involved in teaching music in school and at home to both missionary and Chinese children. She also spent time arranging music for choirs and for worship in the local church. After the Communist victory in 1949, Stella and Nelson were among the last group of RCA missionaries to leave China. They departed the country in 1951 and moved to the Philippines to work among Chinese refugees who had settled there. Retiring from the mission field in 1957, the Veenschotens moved to west Michigan upon their return from the Philippines to be near their youngest daughter, Elin, and her children.[14] Stella continued to compose, translate, and arrange music for the church until she passed away on August 14, 1962, at the age of 70.[15] Her three children and former students wrote about the deep loss that her death was to Chinese Christians and the music community. As stated in her obituary in *The Church Herald,* Stella was known throughout her life for being an "ideal homemaker" and for her musical talent.[16]

In quite different ways, Joyce Angus also fulfilled her Christian calling to China and to her family. Agnes J. Buikema Angus, who went by "Joyce,"

---

11. Girard Veenschoten, "Mother," 20 May 2014, folder "Biographical—Stella Girard Veenschoten, 1939-2014," Henry M. Veenschoten Papers, W88-1078, Joint Archives of Holland, Holland, MI. Against the usual convention of referring to historical figures by their last names, I intentionally refer to Henry M. Veenschoten by his nickname, "Nelson," in order to clarify which Veenschoten I am referring to and avoid implying that a female or male missionary is above the other.

12. Girard Veenschoten, "Memories of Henry and Stella Veenschoten," folder "Biographical—Henry and Stella Veenschoten Vignettes by Girard Veenschoten, October 5, 2011," Henry M. Veenschoten Papers.

13. Formerly known as Changchow or Chiang-chiu, one of the mission stations of the Amoy Mission.

14. Joann Hill, "Stella Girard Veenschoten," folder "Obituaries, correspondence, biographical sketch, funeral bulletin and message—Regarding the death of Stella Veenschoten, August 14, 1962," Henry M. Veenschoten Papers.

15. Elin Avin Veenschoten Moerland, "Stella Elda Girard Veenschoten, August 16, 2007," folder "Biographical—Stella Girard Veenschoten, 1939-2014."

16. Tena Holkeboer, "Mrs. H. M. Veenschoten."

had an experience in China unlike Stella's.[17] Joyce grew up in Grand Rapids, Michigan, and after graduating from high school, got a factory job in Holland, Michigan. After three years, she found herself wanting something more for herself. Her pastor in Grand Rapids told her that he could get her a scholarship to Hope College if she would become a missionary. Joyce agreed, and after graduating from Hope in 1925, she went to the Board of Foreign Missions in New York to receive her commission. It was in the Board's offices that Joyce met William Angus,[18] her future husband. The 1926 annual report of the Board of Foreign Missions listed Joyce as one of the four recruits it appointed to China in the year 1925.[19] The Board had appointed William Angus to the same mission the previous year,[20] and William and Joyce entered the China mission field together in 1925.[21] They studied the Xiamen dialect with the same Chinese language instructor for two years. In 1927, when William Angus passed the language requirement test and was given a position as an evangelist in the mission, Joyce and William were married. In a letter to her parents on June 19, 1927, Stella mentioned the excitement among the missionary families about the approaching wedding of "Miss Buikema."[22] Joyce and William had three children in China during the time they were stationed there—Margery in 1930, David in 1933, and John in 1936.[23] Most of her early years in China were spent balancing her role as a wife and mother with her calling to serve the people of China through the teaching of English.

Joyce's experience as a wife, mother, and missionary in China was marked by the politics of the nation. When war broke out between the United States and Japan following the attack on Pearl Harbor in December

17. I intentionally refer to Agnes J. Buikema Angus by her preferred name, "Joyce," for the reasons stated above regarding the use of names in this chapter.

18. David Angus, interview by Marc Baer, et al. I intentionally refer to William Angus by his first name, William, for the reasons stated above regarding the use of names in this chapter.

19. Reformed Church in America, *Ninety-fourth Annual Report of the Board of Foreign Missions*, pictures between pages xx and xxi, 1.

20. Reformed Church in America, *Ninety-third Annual Report of the Board of Foreign Missions*, pictures between pages xxii and xxiii, xxv.

21. Reformed Church in America, *Ninety-fourth Annual Report of the Board of Foreign Missions*, 1.

22. Stella Veenschoten to Mr. and Mrs. Frank Girard, 19 June 1927, folder "Correspondence—From Stella to her parents, Mr. and Mrs. Frank Girard, 1917–1940," Henry M. Veenschoten Papers.

23. David Angus, interview by Marc Baer, et al.

1941, Japanese forces occupied the island of Gulangyu and interned her and her three children along with several other members of the Amoy Mission until their repatriation to the United States in the summer of 1942. At the time these events took place, William was working in the interior of China, which remained under Chinese control. Thus, the Angus family experienced separation for the duration of the war.[24] The missionary life was hard on many wives and families, and Joyce's experience was an example of the strength that women needed in times of separation to maintain their dual callings to China and their families. Joyce continued to teach English throughout her time in China and managed her household so that her husband could preach the Gospel away from home. The Angus family returned permanently to the United States in 1951, among the last group of RCA missionaries to leave China. Joyce and William were recommissioned and sent to the Philippines, where they remained until William's retirement in 1967. The couple then settled in Orange City, Iowa, near the campus of Northwestern College, where they opened their home to international students from Fujian province who were studying at the college. They continued to minister in this way until Joyce's death in 1974. William established a scholarship in her name at Northwestern; his name was added to the memorial scholarship when he passed away in 1984. The Angus house then became part of the Northwestern campus.[25]

Ruth Holleman, like the other two women, used her talents and position to spread the Gospel in China.[26] Born Ruth Eleanor Vanden Berg in Holland, Michigan, to Reverend Albertus Vanden Berg and his wife, she graduated from Hope College in 1914 and started teaching high school in Zeeland, Michigan. In 1918, Ruth met and married Dr. Clarence Holleman, and in 1919, the Board sent them to the Amoy Mission for Clarence to serve as a medical missionary.[27] When the Hollemans arrived in China, they were assigned to the city of Longyan, where Clarence started treating Chinese patients in a dispensary converted from an old Chinese ancestral

---

24. De Jong, *The Reformed Church in China*, 271–2.

25. David Angus, "A tribute to Dr. William Angus and his wife, Joyce, by their son and their friends," ca. 1984, folder "Biographical, 1956, 1974, n.d.," William R. Angus Papers, H00–1381, Joint Archives of Holland, Holland, MI.

26. I intentionally refer to Ruth Vanden Berg Holleman by her first name for the reasons stated above regarding the use of names in this chapter.

27. I intentionally refer to Clarence H. Holleman by his first name for the reasons stated above regarding the use of names in this chapter.

hall.[28] Ruth set up a girls' school but often also acted as a nurse for her husband during surgery. During their time in China, the Holleman family frequently changed locations due to the unsettled political scene in the country. At one point, they spent time in Zhangzhou, where Ruth and Stella met and became good friends largely because their children were close in age. While Clarence ministered to the Chinese people in their medical needs, Ruth worked wherever she was needed in each city where they lived. After they left China in 1950, the Hollemans settled in California, where Clarence started a private practice. In 1957, they were invited to Taiwan, where they served at the Mackay Memorial Hospital until their retirement in 1960. Ruth passed away in Pomona, California, on April 1, 1966.[29]

The missionary culture in China at the time was very communal, and all the missionaries knew each other and were in close communication. Married missionaries felt a call to the mission field both as couples and as individuals. The three missionary wives—Stella, Joyce, and Ruth—interacted with one another often. They shared the same struggle to balance their home life and their work in China, and they helped one another with emotional support and even material support in times of need. They also knew and interacted with other missionary wives of the mission who were their contemporaries. They did not serve in the same mission station and hence did not live close to each other, but they often opened their doors to one another when one family came to another's mission station, or when their families went to Gulangyu for annual mission meetings. Missionary wives experienced the same political turmoil affecting China as their husbands and lived in the tension between caring for a family and missionary service in China. Stella's letters often gave news of the other missionary wives and affirmed the importance of the camaraderie they shared.

Even though one may speak of the tension between caring for a family and engaging in mission work in China, Stella, Joyce, and Ruth each clearly saw the role of the homemaker in the mission field as part of their calling. Missionary wives were responsible for four principal "household" tasks while in the mission field—moving or relocating the entire family, managing the household staff, homeschooling the children, and maintaining an "American" house. The missionary wife also had to deal with the pressure of completing these tasks alone while her husband was away from

---

28. De Jong, *The Reformed Church in China*, 239. Longyan was formerly referred to as Leng-na by RCA missionaries.

29. "Mrs. Clarence H. Holleman," *The Church Herald*, 1 April 1966.

home during times of unrest, often not knowing if he might be captured by bandits or suffer a worse fate.

The task of moving a household to a mission station or back to the United States for furlough was no easy feat for a missionary wife. Chinese technology was not at the same level of advancement as in the West during this period. In addition, moving from Xiamen to an up-country station in Longyan or Zhangzhou, for example, involved more than a day's journey by channel boat and sedan chair. A typical missionary family moved at least once a year based on the season, the political situation in China, or the type of work in which the husband was engaged. For instance, the Holleman family moved far less than the Veenschoten and Angus families because Clarence was a doctor and, after an initial period in Longyan, supervised the hospital in Xiamen and the Hope and Wilhelmina Hospital on Gulangyu, whereas William and Nelson were itinerant evangelists. In addition, missionaries in China often moved into the mountain regions during the summer months to escape the rising temperatures of southern China. The Veenschotens had a summer cottage built on Da Mao Mountain, to which the family moved during the summer months to get away from the unbearably humid heat and relax.[30] When the time came to move, the missionary wife went to work. The lack of technology made moving a household from one location to another—sometimes up the mountain to a summer home, as did the Veenschotens—particularly difficult. The missionary wife packed up her family's belongings into crates and trunks and shipped whatever she could to the new location. Depending on the distance, geographical features, and the political conditions at the time, the crates and trunks often reached the destination long after the family had arrived. Relocating their families from place to place consumed much of the missionary wives' time and effort.

Along with organizing the relocation of their families as dictated by the demands of the missionary life, the wives also had to adapt to and oversee their household staff. American missionaries in China often lived more comfortably in China than people of comparable economic status did in the United States, for the currency exchange rate was favorable to Americans. Thus, it was commonplace for missionary households to employ several servants. There were three types of household helpers—cooks, "coolies," and "amahs." Cooks were hired to prepare meals for the family; however,

---

30. Girard Veenschoten, "Memories of Henry and Stella Veenschoten." Da Mao was known to the missionaries as Toa-bo in the Xiamen dialect.

this was complicated for many missionary wives. Chinese cooks could not just be put to work because these women insisted that they make American dishes for their families. Cooks had to be trained by missionary wives and taught American recipes. In Stella's letters to her parents, she often wrote about the trouble of finding a good cook willing to learn American cuisine. The second type of household staff was a "coolie." A missionary household generally had one or two coolies at a given time. In the American tradition, these servants would have been called "laborers." They did the heavy lifting for the women when their husbands were away; they also carried supplies and served as guides for male missionaries on evangelistic trips. The third type of servant was the "amah," who was a nanny for the children of missionaries and especially important for the missionary wives. The amahs gave the missionary wives some freedom to engage in activities outside the home, especially while their husbands were away for weeks on evangelistic trips.

However, managing Chinese servants proved to have its own challenges. Stella wrote often to her parents, not only about the difficulty of finding good household staff, but also about how much she would have preferred not to have them around the house: "I tell you I would fire every one of them if I could. It sounds so big to most people at home when we say, 'Oh, we keep three servants.' Well you can just believe me, I prefer the kind of servants we have at home: vacuum cleaner, electric washers, iron, gas stove, running water and such like."[31] Other wives felt this way about their household staff as well. The desire to maintain an "American home" will be discussed below, but the point here is that the household staff was necessary to maintaining the missionary wife's household vision. Another purpose of employing a household staff was the freedom and mobility it gave to these missionary wives in a foreign country. While many of the wives took language lessons with their husbands before being assigned to a mission station, they were still rather unaccustomed to the culture of the marketplace and other locations they needed to visit for errands and various day-to-day responsibilities. The household staff thus facilitated the mobility of these women and their attempts to navigate the culture and language of the Chinese people.[32] Although the amahs were vital for the life of a missionary family, they posed many obstacles to the "American

---

31. Stella Veenschoten to Mrs. Frank Girard, 18 February 1923, folder "Correspondence—From Stella to her parents, Mr. and Mrs. Frank Girard, 1917–1940."
32. David Angus, interview by Marc Baer et al.

household" that the missionary wives worked tirelessly to build. The missionary wives wanted to give their children an American upbringing. However, the cultural differences between China and America were particularly noticeable in childrearing practices, and Chinese women's indulgent attitude toward boys could frustrate an American mother's efforts to discipline her son. Although the help of servants was much needed in the household, these American women did not want them to influence their children and wanted to safeguard the "American" culture within their homes.

The responsibilities that the missionary wives carried were therefore aimed at keeping the home as "American" as possible. It appears that missionaries sought to avoid assimilation by Chinese culture for their children's sake. David, son of Joyce and William Angus, recalled that the missionary culture in China placed great importance on bringing up children as "Americans."[33] Criticisms of "cultural imperialism" are often hurled at missionaries; their evangelistic efforts are commonly perceived as attempts to impose their own beliefs and home cultures upon an indigenous population, or worse, as preparation for political and economic encroachments by their home governments or compatriots. In his article "Beyond Cultural Imperialism," Ryan Dunch argues that the missionary movement should be considered in light of the larger process of modern cultural globalization, and that the concept of cultural imperialism is "too blunt an instrument for analyzing this process."[34] As Stella's example shows, the missionary wives were more "defensive" than "imperialistic" in their relationship to the Chinese culture around them. In the end, the missionary wives were rearing their children in the expectation that they needed to be prepared to integrate into American society when it came time to return to America. This necessarily involved home-schooling the children in their early years. An important aspect of these women's experiences as they brought up their children was what one would call "single parenting" in our day. Stella, Joyce, and Ruth all experienced extended stretches on their own when they were without the help of their husbands. This was a more frequent occurrence for the wives of husbands who were itinerant evangelists. William and Nelson often went out into the countryside to visit remote villages for two or more weeks at a time. In her letters, Stella constantly talked about when Nelson would return or when he was leaving again—the life of a

---

33. David Angus, interview by Marc Baer et al.
34. Dunch, "Beyond Cultural Imperialism," 325.

missionary wife was often lonely because of the extended periods of time spent by themselves with the children.

Moreover, during times of political unrest, missionaries could be captured by bandits or soldiers. Stella, Joyce, and Ruth all had their share of such uncertain situations. Yet, each woman's ability to be calm in a crisis and maintain her faith in God is striking. Ruth and Clarence, for instance, fled Longyan in 1929 when Communist forces briefly occupied the city. Soldiers captured Clarence, but Ruth and their children managed to reach Zhangzhou, and from there traveled to Gulangyu. Clarence escaped on the fifth day of his capture, went into hiding for two days, and then stayed with friends for nearly three weeks before making his way to Gulangyu to reunite with Ruth and their children.[35] Likewise, events following the outbreak of war between Japan and the United States in December 1941 tested the courage of Stella and Joyce. When Nelson returned to China from furlough in America in November 1941, Stella and their children stayed behind in America due to the uncertain world situation of the time. Immediately after Japan's attack on Pearl Harbor on December 7, Nelson, Joyce and the Angus children, and other RCA missionaries who were then on the island of Gulangyu were interned by Japanese forces in houses owned by the mission. Meanwhile, William was itinerating up-country. Thus, both the Veenschotens and the Anguses experienced family separation. Joyce and the Angus children were repatriated in June 1942, and Nelson not until September 1943, in prisoner exchanges between the United States and Japan.[36]

For almost two years, Stella had no communication with Nelson. Yet, she calmly and faithfully played her role in the home as a missionary wife. In correspondence with William, who was in free China at the time, Stella received some information regarding the well-being of the missionaries interned on Gulangyu. Although Stella had no word from Nelson throughout his internment, she continued to write to him. Between December 21, 1941, and September 12, 1943, Stella wrote calmly about matters of the

---

35. De Jong, *The Reformed Church in China*, 252–3.

36. De Jong, *The Reformed Church in China*, 271–8; Henry M. Veenschoten, interview by Donald Hill, 5 December 1971, transcript, 22–8, Old China Hands Oral History Project, Hope College Digital Commons, https://digitalcommons.hope.edu/old_china/13/ (accessed 27 June 2019); William Angus, interview by David M. Vander Haar, 16 & 17 September 1976, transcript, 28, Old China Hands Oral History Project, Hope College Digital Commons, https://digitalcommons.hope.edu/old_china/1/ (accessed 27 June 2019).

home to Nelson. In a peaceful and faithful tone, she expressed in her letters her desire to have her husband return safely. Joyce's separation from William was even more prolonged. For even though she was repatriated in 1942, William could not return from China until after the end of the war. When an interviewer in the 1970s commented that it was a long time to be separated, William said in stoic missionary fashion, "Yes. We were separated for four and a half years."[37] For these missionary wives, an integral part of their calling was the uncertainty and potential danger that they and their loved ones faced.

Important as providing a home for her husband was, every missionary wife also found a way to utilize her specific talents and gifts to serve the people of China. The examples of Stella, Joyce, and Ruth show how missionary wives did this through music, education, and medicine. Music was a powerful and important ministry tool that some missionaries used to spread the Gospel to the people of China. Across the world, music in the church forms an important part of any worship service, and the missionary wives who were able to minister in this way helped the church grow. As a trained musician, Stella often spent hours at the piano—composing, singing, and playing. As her children grew older, she became more and more involved in her music as a ministry to the Chinese people. She taught piano and voice lessons to not only missionary children but also Chinese Christians. As she gained more time away from the home, she began teaching music in various mission schools. Her work as a musician and her talents as a teacher, singer, pianist, and composer came to be well-known in the missionary community. In addition to her work as a music teacher, Stella was also in charge of the worship music and played the piano at the church in Zhangzhou, or wherever the family was stationed at the time. In these ways, Stella answered her call to the mission field.

As for Joyce, she first went to the mission field as a single woman. Her assignment was to teach English. When she and William started their family as a young missionary couple in China, the responsibilities of childrearing became primary. Likewise, Ruth played her role as a missionary by not only bringing up children but also assisting Clarence in surgery during their early years in China. From the Japanese invasion of Xiamen in 1938 to the internment of the missionaries in 1941, Ruth assisted Clarence in running a clinic that provided milk for refugee babies. The dual roles of the

---

37. William Angus, interview by David M. Vander Haar, 16 & 17 September 1976, transcript, 28.

missionary wife in the family and in the mission field were both valuable and important. The family dictated the amount and type of work that the missionary wife could do for China. In all three women's situations, as their children became older and left home to attend school elsewhere in China or in America, the women took on more tasks and responsibilities in the mission field. Stella began teaching more classes and traveling to other villages to sing and play music. Joyce began to teach more and travel with her husband on evangelistic missions. And Ruth started working in the hospital again and created programs to meet the needs of the Chinese people in wartime. Somehow, the three women found their own balance between the conflicting demands of home and mission field, but the tension between the two was nonetheless real. As Hunter observes,

> The cultural conservatism fostered by child-rearing responsibilities limited the relationships of American mothers with China and with their work. Most women found it difficult simultaneously to sustain a secure American homelife for children within compound walls and to embrace the innovation and experiment of a working life outside the home. Women who had confidently envisioned their work as a female contribution to the global expansion of Christian influence found that, instead, their responsibilities led to their participation in a defensive domesticity at home.[38]

As the examples of Stella, Joyce, and Ruth show, only as time went on could missionary wives reconcile the conflicting demands of the home and the mission field, both integral to their sense of calling. In the beginning of these married women's missionary careers, family responsibilities were the most pressing and important. The missionary wife had to take care of the children, maintain a household, secure her children's education, and more, as she endeavored to establish her own place in the mission. There was not a distinct, singular role for the missionary wife as there was for a doctor or an evangelist, which gave these women freedom to shape their own roles in China. With persistence, missionary wives established their roles by employing their individual talents and gifts, and, as their children grew older, the pressing needs of their families decreased. Missionary wives were an indispensable part of the greater story of the Gospel in China. Although the number of sources that depict their lives and work is limited, their footprints can still be discerned. Difficult as it was, Stella, Joyce, and Ruth found ways to live out the call of the Gospel: "Therefore go and make disciples of

---

38. Jane Hunter, *The Gospel of Gentility*, 112.

all nations, baptizing them in the name of the Father and of the Son and of the Holy Spirit, and teaching them to obey everything I have commanded you. And surely I am with you always, to the very end of the age."[39]

Bibliography

Primary Sources

Angus, David. Interview. July 21, 2014.
Henry M. Veenschoten Papers. W88-1078. Joint Archives of Holland, Holland, MI.
"Old China Hands Oral History Project." Hope College Digital Commons. https://digitalcommons.hope.edu/old_china/.
Reformed Church in America. *Ninety-fourth Annual Report of the Board of Foreign Missions of the Reformed Church in America*. New York: The Abbott Press, 1926.
William R. Angus Jr. Papers. H00-1381. Joint Archives of Holland, Holland, MI.

Secondary Sources

Cox, Jeffrey. *The British Missionary Enterprise since 1700*. Christianity and Society in the Modern World. New York: Routledge, 2010.
De Jong, Gerald F. *The Reformed Church in China, 1842–1951*. Historical Series of the Reformed Church in America 22. Grand Rapids: Eerdmans, 1992.
Dunch, Ryan. "Beyond Cultural Imperialism: Cultural Theory, Christian Missions, and Global Modernity." *History and Theory* 41/3 (2002) 301–25.
Hunter, Jane. *The Gospel of Gentility: American Women Missionaries in Turn-of-the-Century China*. New Haven: Yale University Press, 1984.

---

39. Matt 28:19–20 (NIV).

4

HOPE AND WILHELMINA HOSPITAL SCHOOL OF NURSING

The Role of Missionary Nurses in Xiamen, China

KATELYN DICKERSON

JEANNETTE VELDMAN WAS A missionary nurse of the Reformed Church in America (RCA) during the early twentieth century. Her work in Xiamen, China, where she was stationed, served as the foundation for Hope and Wilhelmina Hospital School of Nursing. Veldman and her fellow missionary nurses were extremely passionate about the training of young Chinese nurses in a country that had yet to embrace the nursing profession. Many of her contemporaries questioned her decision to practice and teach nursing in China. She responded as follows:

> Is Christian nursing in China worthwhile? When God fills your heart so full of His peace and love that it fairly bursts, is it worthwhile? When a body is saved, is it worthwhile? When a new soul grasps the meaning of the free gift of love, is it worthwhile? Broken bodies repaired, broken hearts mended, lost hopes replenished, lost souls brought to Christ. Friends, those are the results of the work of yours and my hospital.[1]

1. Jeannette Veldman to Friends, 6 September 1932, folder "Correspondence,

Hope and Wilhelmina Hospital School of Nursing faithfully served its students, the hospital, and the local community from 1924, when missionary nurse Jean Nienhuis first began training student nurses, until its service was interrupted by World War II. The school's history spans two periods: the first, starting in 1924 and ending in 1941, was the most fruitful time of the school, hence the period discussed in this paper. The second period was much shorter, lasting from 1946, when the school reopened following Japan's surrender the year before, to 1951. The years during which the school operated proved to be crucial to women's social and professional progress in China. The Christian missionaries who founded the nursing school challenged the boundaries of both the medical profession and women's place in society. Their progressive spirit and Christian ideals enabled their student nurses and graduates to do the same.

The Founding of Hope and Wilhelmina Hospital School of Nursing

It is imperative to understand the formative years of both the hospital and the nursing school because of the foundation that they provided to the school in its peak years. Dr. John Otte began the construction of Hope Hospital in 1897, with funds that he had raised during his furlough in America. The hospital was dedicated and started receiving patients in 1898.[2] It was located on the small island of Gulangyu, about a mile away from the larger island of Xiamen; the city of Xiamen in Fujian province, China, encompassed both islands, which figured prominently in the work of the Amoy Mission of the RCA.[3] Hope Hospital was originally designed as a men's hospital, but a women's facility was soon integrated into the premises. The women's hospital was funded by and subsequently named after Queen Wilhelmina of the Netherlands.[4] Dr. Otte's persistence and hard work quickly

---

1930–1934," Jeannette Veldman Papers, W89-1012, Joint Archives of Holland, Holland, MI.

2. MacGillivray, *A Century of Protestant Missions in China (1807–1907)*, 376. Please see the chapter "A Visionary Mission" by Rebekah Llorens in this volume for the work of Dr. J. A. Otte.

3. The location names have changed since the early twentieth century. During the period that the missionaries lived in China, the city of Xiamen was known as Amoy, and the island of Gulangyu was known as Kulangsu. Quotes in this chapter will reference the traditional names.

4. MacGillivray, *A Century of Protestant Missions in China (1807–1907)*, 376.

bore fruit, and he gained a reputation in the surrounding region for the hospitals' modern technology, clean environment, and outstanding personnel. This was in no small part due to Otte's sincere dedication to the people of Xiamen and his devotion to the mission. There was a lack of formally trained medical personnel at the mission hospitals. Dr. Otte recognized this and began to train willing students in medicine.[5] Thus, from the very beginning, Hope Hospital was known not only as a place of healthcare, but also as an institution of learning.

Before the founding of the nursing school, missionary nurses were already working at the hospital. According to Veldman's "The History of the Hope Hospital School of Nursing," the first nurse to arrive for work on the island was Marie Kranenberg. She arrived around the tenth year into the hospital's existence. In 1914 she was joined by Mena Merman. Both women hailed from the Netherlands and brought with them their traditional Dutch values.[6] These two nurses upheld strict standards. They adhered to clearly stated visiting hours and demanded a spotless facility. The newly adopted restrictions shocked and annoyed their Chinese patients, who were unfamiliar with their styles and expectations.[7] However, despite the new nurses' unfamiliar ways, the number of the hospital's Chinese patients continued to grow. When Kranenberg returned to the Netherlands, the increasing number of patients forced Merman to limit her services to the women's facility, which left the men's section of the hospital in the care of the hospital servants and doctors.[8]

Missionary nurse Jean Nienhuis arrived at Hope and Wilhelmina Hospital in 1920. As the founder of the nursing school, Nienhuis was critical to the school's evolution. She was born and raised in Holland, Michigan, and did her formal training at Blodgett Nursing School in Grand Rapids, Michigan. She was the first trained nurse from America to arrive in

---

5. MacGillivray, *A Century of Protestant Missions in China (1807–1907)*, 377.

6. Jeannette Veldman, "History of the Hope Hospital School of Nursing with Some of Its Human Side" (unpublished manuscript, January 1933), 1, folder "Missions – Amoy (China) – Hope Hospital – General, 1912–1949," Jeannette Veldman Papers. Fellow missionary nurse Jean Nienhuis collaborated with Veldman to create this history and is quoted several times in it by the latter.

7. Jeannette Veldman, "History of the Hope Hospital School of Nursing," 2–3.

8. In the original documents, the term "coolie" was used. It covered all manual laborers, including those who were employed by the hospital. I have chosen to use the term "hospital servants" because of the nature of their work and their position in the hospital.

Xiamen. Nienhuis was given the men's hospital as her initial project.[9] As she continued her work at the hospital in Xiamen, she began to understand the growing need for nurses around the globe, and particularly in China. The conditions that she witnessed during the first few months following her arrival astounded her, but the language barrier she faced made it almost impossible for her to express her grievances to the hospital servants, who worked under her authority. At a later point she remembered, "Everything was dirty. I was afraid to touch anything ... I'd shut myself up in a vacant room and wonder, 'What shall I do?'"[10] Nienhuis's observation was confirmed by the accounts of several other missionary nurses. A mission hospital in China was not a pleasant workplace in the early 1900s. There were only one or two trained nurses to care for the roughly one hundred fifty patients admitted to the hospital at any given time. The nurses only had the hospital servants to rely on as nurses' aides. In addition, they had to work against cultural expectations and without the support of the outside community. This is not to say that the hospitals that missionary nurses worked in were unwelcoming. On the contrary, doctors were often thoroughly grateful for the presence of a missionary nurse in their hospital. Nurses provided a level of care unique to their profession and lightened the heavy burdens placed on the missionary doctors.

In the early twentieth century, nursing as a profession was still in its infancy. Modern nursing is often traced back to Florence Nightingale and the Crimean War in the mid-1800s.[11] Nightingale's book, *Notes on Nursing* (1859), essentially set the guidelines for modern nursing. In the half century after her book gained recognition, nursing took off as a potential career option for young women who were not interested in traditional life paths. Although nursing was becoming a regular profession in the Western medical field, medical missionaries in southern China were just introducing it. At the time, duties that today would be expected of a nurse were divided between the patients' families and hospital servants.[12] The job of a hospital servant was to clean and prepare the hospital for patients. Families took care of their own loved ones who were admitted to the hospital regardless of the length of the hospital stay. Nienhuis set out to change this and to ensure that the medical needs of the patients were successfully met.

9. Veldman, "History of the Hope Hospital School of Nursing," 2.
10. Veldman, "History of the Hope Hospital School of Nursing," 3.
11. Group and Roberts, *Nursing, Physician Control, and the Medical Monopoly*, 81.
12. Veldman, "History of the Hope Hospital School of Nursing," 3–4.

Twenty years after the founding of Hope and Wilhelmina Hospital, Jean Nienhuis encountered great difficulties trying to keep up with the demands of patients. Doctors were learning to depend on nurses like Nienhuis, and the nursing profession was becoming invaluable to the hospital. The doctors' increasing dependence on Nienhuis, coupled with the limited hours in a day, had her "dreaming of taking in girls as students and of beginning a nurses' training school and linking up with the Nurses' Association of China."[13] Nienhuis wanted to improve conditions at the hospital and find a niche for young Chinese women to better themselves and the community. At the start, these goals seemed far-fetched, but after a visit from Cora E. Simpson in 1922, they began to appear more realistic. Simpson, one of the founders of the Nurses' Association of China (NAC), which held its first annual meeting in 1910, was touring southern China to promote the establishment of nurses' training schools. She strengthened Nienhuis's argument for a nursing school by showing her and the other hospital personnel the practicality of such a program. Two years later, Nienhuis began taking in a few students to help her. As the school was not yet recognized by the NAC, students could not receive any formal nursing degree from the school. These students were acting in nursing capacities before any formal degree program was put in place. In 1925, the NAC recognized Hope and Wilhelmina Hospital School of Nursing.[14] With the "official" opening of the nursing school and nurses now occupying a professionally recognized space, the atmosphere of the hospital began to change.

Hope and Wilhelmina Hospital School of Nursing thus originated from the mission hospitals' dire need for trained nurses. By this time, both of the hospital's first two nurses had returned to the Netherlands, leaving Nienhuis on her own. In 1924, a young nurse named Alma Matheison joined Nienhuis, but Matheison left to get married at the end of five years. Nienhuis had the intermittent help of other American nurses in the late 1920s, but it was not until 1931 that two missionary nurses, Jeannette Veldman and Jessie Platz, came to the hospital as permanent co-workers.[15] Collaborating with Nienhuis, the two new nurses would become the heart and soul of the nursing school. Each woman would by turns take on the roles of Director of Nursing and Nursing Student Supervisor during her time at the hospital. The trio ran the nursing school until it was forced to close in 1941.

13. Veldman, "History of the Hope Hospital School of Nursing," 5.
14. Veldman, "History of the Hope Hospital School of Nursing," 7.
15. Veldman, "History of the Hope Hospital School of Nursing," 11.

The Staff and Students of
Hope and Wilhelmina Hospital School of Nursing

Nienhuis, Platz, and Veldman all left their mark on Hope and Wilhelmina Hospital, and on the nursing school in the years leading up to World War II. By creating an intimate bond with their Chinese pupils, the missionary nurses were able to push their students out of their comfort zones. These nurses' presence made it possible for young Chinese women to find their own place in a society that confined women to the home. Invariably, the nursing profession provided a contrast to the traditional roles of Chinese women. The missionary nurses were strong, independent women whose time in Xiamen was only one aspect of their impressive careers. They taught their Chinese students how to be capable Christian nurses, all the while providing strong female role models for their young students to look up to. This mentoring relationship, built upon trust, empowered these young Chinese women to expand their horizons beyond the limits set by the expectations of their time and society.

Nienhuis, Platz, and Veldman led extremely busy lives. In 1932, Veldman took the time to detail a day in her life as a missionary nurse in a letter to her home church. She started each day at 7:00 a.m. by gathering all the nurses on staff for Scripture reading and communal prayers. After the morning prayers, the nurses who had been on night duty gave their reports. Veldman then read out the daily assignment of tasks for each young nurse and sent her to her post. At the time Veldman wrote this account of a typical day, there were nineteen nurses and students under her supervision. This small group of women was at the call of around 125 in-patients at the hospital. Every day, Veldman checked on each of these patients individually, addressing any issues or concerns and determining if they were properly cared for. The seventeen hospital servants employed by the hospital were also under Veldman's authority. She double-checked all areas of the hospital to ensure that the facility was being properly maintained. Since both the hospital servants and the nurses reported to her, Veldman also had the responsibility of responding to their complaints or requests. In addition, she performed administrative tasks such as checking for missing supplies, sending in requisitions, and monitoring the laundry, all while supervising her pupils and teaching intermittently throughout the day. At the end of each day, Veldman made sure that the lights were off by 10:00 p.m.[16] All in

---

16. Veldman to Friends, 6 September 1932.

all, the missionary nurses oversaw the welfare of both the nursing school's students and all of the hospital's patients.

The American nurses' responsibilities at the mission hospital did not end with teaching, administrative, and medical work. The missionary nurses were also called to evangelization. While in China, their main goal was to lead Chinese to the Christian faith. This sentiment was expressed by Veldman in a report, in which she stated that the nursing school's goal was "to develop the student's spiritual side in order that she derive pleasure from the beauty of true service."[17] Thus, the missionary nurses had to consider an extra dimension in their work of teaching and caring for patients. The dedication of doctors and nurses to Christian ideals made mission hospitals a location where many conversions took place. People who needed care at a hospital were often at their most vulnerable and were sometimes more open to alternative belief systems. Veldman observed that many of the Christians whom she met in China told her that they had first heard the Gospel in a hospital.[18] In fact, this Christian influence extended to the student nurses as well. In an article written after the nursing school closed for the first time, Veldman recounted an incident involving one of her students, to whom she had given the name Gladys. Gladys was not a Christian when she first came to the nursing school. Once she accidentally allowed an infant to roll off a weighing scale. Although the child was unharmed, the young student nurse was shaken and terrified by the prospect of admitting the mistake to Veldman. Veldman responded sternly because of the seriousness of the accident, but she was also calm and ultimately forgiving. Weeks later, Gladys came to Veldman's office to express her desire to become a Christian. She gave this as her reason: "I was terribly frightened and worried, but you were calm and gentle and displayed only a loving and understanding heart. I knew then that there was something to being a Christian."[19] This conversion story was a testament to both the professionalism and faith of the missionary nurses. Gladys was not one of the patients, stricken ill and lying in a hospital bed. She was a busy, professional woman who was drawn to Christianity by the work and attitude of the missionary nurses.

17. Report, "Nursing Department, School of Nursing," 1949, typescript, folder "Missions – Amoy (China) – Hope Hospital – General, 1912–1949."

18. Jeannette Veldman to Friends, 16 May 1932, folder "Correspondence, 1930–1934."

19. Jeannette Veldman, "In the Most Unconscious Way. . .," *The Church Herald*, 28 September 1945.

While the missionary nurses were training their students to become nurses, they also intended to pave the way for Chinese nurses to maintain their own hospitals and schools at some point not too far in the future. Intertwined with these goals for transforming the medical profession in China were a certain vision of womanhood that the missionary nurses wished to impart to their pupils. The missionary nurses believed that the nursing profession required women of a certain set of qualities. In the report of the nursing school mentioned previously, another stated goal was "to develop the student's social nature and help her build up [a] pleasing and interesting personality and to help her make adjustments to the ever-changing demands of life."[20] This goal proved difficult to accomplish because of the cultural norms that the nursing community had to contend with. The missionary nurses' spoken or unspoken goal of encouraging Chinese nurses to challenge the boundaries placed upon them by society met with great resistance from the students. Social norms were deeply engrained in the students as well as the community where the hospital and nursing school were located. Because entering the profession was itself a courageous act, a student could hardly be expected to do all that the missionary nurses thought was necessary. As Veldman acknowledged, nursing in China required "girls with a somewhat adventurous, unselfish, sacrificing spirit. . . as the community as a whole gave them very little, if any, respect."[21] The profession itself already demanded a great deal of courage from the young Chinese women.

The nursing students were already breaking boundaries simply by being students. The missionary nurses could not force their pupils to go further than they were willing to do in challenging the social expectations of their day. Once their training was completed, the newly minted Chinese nurses had to continue to be pioneers in their own way. They had to be the ones promoting their profession and role as women in Chinese society, for the missionaries could not do this for them. Sometimes, missionary leadership was more a hindrance than a facilitator in the process of developing Chinese leadership. In the article "Breaking into Public Service," John Watt argues that women nurses in China struggled to establish their profession in part because of their reliance on foreign missionary leaders. From the

20. Report, "Nursing Department, School of Nursing."
21. Veldman to Friends, 16 May 1932.

very beginning, hospitals and organizations such as the NAC were run by foreigners, leaving little room for Chinese nurses to govern themselves.[22]

Watt's analysis is applicable to the context in which the Chinese nurses at Hope and Wilhelmina Hospital learned the skills of the profession and served. They were studying and working at a mission hospital run by foreigners. Missionary nurses managed the nursing school as well as the hospital's Chinese and Western nurses, and the superintendent of the hospital was a missionary doctor. Some graduate nurses did have leadership positions such as night supervisor or teaching supervisor, but as late as 1940 none ever reached the top positions held by the missionary nurses.[23] This disparity ultimately limited the full advancement of Chinese nurses while missionary nurses were still in China. Even so, the lack of Chinese leadership never developed into a contentious issue at Hope and Wilhelmina Hospital and the nursing school. There was no power struggle and no spite on the part of the missionaries; the hospital was simply maintaining the status quo. Missionaries had founded the hospital in the late nineteenth century and later had established the nursing school. Foreigners had always been in charge because of the hospital's background and ties to the mission. Although delegating more authority to the Chinese personnel would have benefited the hospital and nursing school in the long run, the missionaries ran the institutions effectively and did not actively assign top leadership roles to the Chinese. As Watt points out, Chinese leaders in the nursing community would have been more adept at understanding the psychology of their patients and comforting them than a foreigner.[24] In the missionaries' perception, however, the missionary nurses' leadership positions in the hospital and nursing school were not a roadblock but a stepping-stone to the self-sufficiency of the Chinese women under their supervision. Their role as leaders was to facilitate an eventual succession by their Chinese pupils.

The missionary nurses were very dedicated to their pupils and developed a strong bond with many of them. The American nurses lived together with their students in the Nurses' Home. They said their daily prayers and

22. John Watt, "Breaking into Public Service: The Development of Nursing in Modern China, 1870–1949," *Nursing History Review* 12 (2004) 71.

23. "Annual Report of Hope and Wilhelmina Hospital, Kulangsu, Amoy, China, for 1939 and 1940," 1–2, folder "Annual Report of Hope and Wilhelmina Hospital, Amoy Mission, 1938–1940, 1949," China Mission Papers 1888–1979, W88-0315, Joint Archives of Holland.

24. Watt, "Breaking into Public Service," 71.

studied the Bible together. Because of the nature of nursing, a professional and academic hierarchy existed at the hospital. Nonetheless, socially and religiously, all the nurses were on an equal footing. The missionary nurses created an environment that allowed for cross-cultural interaction. Starting in 1933, Nienhuis and Veldman threw an annual Christmas party for all the students and nurses.[25] Together the Chinese and American nurses planned events such as a celebration of Florence Nightingale and weekly Bible studies for the students. Thus, the missionary nurses introduced another way of building relationships that was not based strictly on kinship and was less hierarchical than was prevalent during that time in China.

One reason why the Chinese and American nurses were able to develop this close relationship was the requirement that missionary nurses spend an entire year in language study before taking up hospital assignments. By the end of that first year, the language proficiency of the nurses was good enough for them to converse with their students. This was an important step taken by the missionary nurses to immerse themselves in their students' culture and actively cultivate a meaningful relationship with their students. Even so, friendship of the kind between equals did not come naturally. A letter from a student nurse to Nienhuis evidenced the uncertainty experienced by this young Chinese in her relationship with the teacher: "Thank you very much with all my heart for the love you have given me and I want to be one of your good friends."[26] In fact, Miss Gim-siu Sio, the student nurse, began her letter with both tender affection and self-consciousness at addressing Nienhuis by her first name: "Dear friend, Jean, I find myself have the courage to call you 'Jean.' Are you surprised?" Unusual as they were, when such cross-cultural friendships did develop, they greatly enriched the lives of both individuals and were cherished by them throughout their lives.

By far the most commonly expressed emotion on the part of former students of the nursing school was gratitude. Decades after the end of the missionary era in China, former missionaries and missionary children were finally able to return to Xiamen for visits. "[Chinese] women that had gone through the program were so grateful for their education, whenever elderly [missionary] nurses returned they were showered with gifts and parties,"

---

25. Jeannette Veldman to John Veldman, 16 December 1933, folder "Correspondence, 1930–1934," Jeannette Veldman Papers.

26. Gim-siu Sio to Jean Nienhuis, 14 May 1933, folder "Correspondence, 1921–1939," Jean Nienhuis Papers, W96-1208, Joint Archives of Holland.

recalled David Angus, son of RCA missionary William Angus.[27] Veldman was one of those who received a loving and grateful welcome when she visited Xiamen in the 1980s.[28] Chinese nurses trained by medical missionaries were given an invaluable education, which included professional skills that could be used for a lifetime. Indeed, Chinese nurses who had been trained by Hope and Wilhelmina Hospital School of Nursing appreciated the work of the missionary nurses and remained grateful throughout their lives.

Hope and Wilhelmina Hospital School of Nursing and Social Change in China

The introduction of the nursing profession in China, of which Hope and Wilhelmina Hospital School of Nursing was a picture, brought about several social changes in Chinese society. Both the standards of and attitudes toward the profession evolved in the course of the existence of the nursing school. One of the most visible changes was the dress code. Back in the early 1920s, before the school was registered with the NAC, there was hardly a prescribed way of dress for nurses. The student nurses wore traditional Chinese shirts and pants with assorted colors of stockings and shoes to class and work.[29] By the time the school was accredited, the missionary nurses had begun to enforce a dress code. Veldman recounted that at first the students were only required to wear short straight blouses and trousers, all white.[30] With regard to the rest of their attire, she stated that they were allowed to wear "[s]hoes and stockings still as they pleased—one step at a time is all one takes when first learning to walk—no caps."[31] In fact, the subject of uniforms was under constant debate over the years, because caps were socially unacceptable, and the color white was associated with mourning. In 1927, they changed once again to the long white Chinese dress for student nurses, which allowed patients to distinguish between student

---

27. David Angus, interview by Marc Baer, Claire Barrett, Katelyn Dickerson, Victoria Longfield, and Gloria Tseng, 21 July 2014, Hope College, Holland, MI.

28. Jeannette Veldman to Dear Ones, 14 August 1985, folder "Correspondence, 1984–1985," Jeannette Veldman Papers.

29. Veldman, "History of the Hope Hospital School of Nursing," 13.

30. Veldman, "History of the Hope Hospital School of Nursing," 13.

31. Veldman, "History of the Hope Hospital School of Nursing," 13.

nurses and fully trained nurses more easily.[32] By the early 1930s, the NAC had set its own standard, requiring all student nurses to wear a specific uniform. It consisted of "a short blue Chinese blouse covered with a long sleeveless and collarless white Chinese-style apron, a cap, either black shoes and hose, or white shoes and hose, very attractive, practical and neat."[33] Although the uniform required by the NAC included a cap, the students of Hope and Wilhelmina Hospital School of Nursing fought vehemently against wearing white caps. As the most contentious issue between missionary nurses and their students at the nursing school, the nurse's uniform was a visible representation of the social changes brought about by the nursing profession.

More profound changes took place in nurse-patient relations, particularly in their departure from traditional gender norms. In the early twentieth century, strict rules still regulated how a young woman should and should not interact with a man. For the most part, women were not to interact with any man who was not a family relation. Nursing pushed against this traditional boundary in order to serve every patient. A nurse was expected to maintain the health and care of her patients regardless of their race, religion, and sex. Unfortunately, due to the cultural norms of the time, for many years patient care in the men's hospital could not be held to the same standard as in the women's hospital. The young nurses refused to enter the men's hospital, let alone touch and care for an unknown man.[34] Male patients also, initially, resisted contact with the nurses. The obstacle of traditional gender norms proved difficult to overcome, even more so than getting student nurses to observe the dress code. Chinese girls were taught from a young age their place in society, and with arranged marriages being the norm, they normally did not need to interact with men outside their families until they married.[35] Parents did not want their daughters to risk their innocence for becoming a nurse, for nursing had yet to be accepted as a respectable profession for young women. Most student nurses did not dare enter the men's hospital. Few were willing to challenge the gender barrier, even with the encouragement of the missionary nurses.

It took women who were willing to take risks to break down the gender barrier in patient care, and one gets a glimpse of the strength this required

---

32. Veldman, "History of the Hope Hospital School of Nursing," 13.
33. Veldman, "History of the Hope Hospital School of Nursing," 13.
34. Veldman, "History of the Hope Hospital School of Nursing," 15.
35. Veldman, "History of the Hope Hospital School of Nursing," 15

in one of the student nurses whose experiences Veldman recounted. To avoid criticism from her peers, she carried out her duties in the men's hospital only upon express orders from her supervisors. Since direct orders from the head nurses could not be disobeyed, they shielded the student nurse from peer pressure to some extent. Even so, Veldman remarked, "She sometimes loses hope—the students are not yet willing to follow her example—but she goes on in response to what she believes [to be] the call of Christ."[36] Only gradually over the years was the nursing school able to get more of its students to commit to work in the men's hospital.

The leaders of the nursing school took gradual steps to get their pupils to accept work in the men's hospital. One of the first tasks that Nienhuis, Veldman, and Platz had their students do was to distribute pills to the male patients. They then moved on to taking temperatures and pulses, which was a huge step for both the school and the student nurses.[37] The next step was to have the students feed some male patients and provide some minor treatments. Each move toward full care for male patients was met with resistance from the student nurses, but the teachers persisted. What took place at Hope and Wilhelmina Hospital School of Nursing was a small picture of women's progress in early twentieth-century China, including advancement in female education. Ultimately, Chinese women themselves had to be the ones blazing a new trail for women in China.

Over time, classroom instruction at the nursing school also evolved. During the first few years of the school's existence, the curriculum consisted of basic health classes and home economics.[38] It was a means to continue the young women's general education as they trained to be nurses. Since most of the pupils in the program had not reached the ninth grade, the missionary nurses of the nursing school and the NAC considered it necessary to provide them with basic education. By the late 1930s, students were studying science-based subjects such as dietetics, gynecology, bacteriology, and communicable diseases, as well as taking courses such as the history of nursing, nursing ethics, psychology, and Chinese citizenship.[39] With regard to practical skills, the young women started their training right

36. Veldman, "History of the Hope Hospital School of Nursing," 16.

37. Veldman, "History of the Hope Hospital School of Nursing," 16.

38. "Annual Report of Hope and Wilhelmina Hospital, Kulangsu, Amoy, China, for 1939 and 1940," 6.

39. Play, written by the student nurses of Hope and Wilhelmina Hospital and performed at the hospital's open house on 5 May 1939, Act 6, folder "Missions – Amoy (China) – Hope Hospital – Student Play, 1939," Jeannette Veldman Papers.

away in the hospital. As Platz recalled, "They had to do the same work I did ... we had a regular schedule just like public health nurses have in this country [America]."[40] The development of a more demanding curriculum was an indication of the changing status of nurses in China during the early twentieth century. Nurses were assuming an increasingly prominent role in medical care and therefore had to have an ever-larger skill set; hence, an increasingly advanced curriculum was required for their training.

After discovering the practical benefits of having nurses in the hospital, doctors became the main supporters of the nurses' presence. Both missionary and Chinese doctors assisted in the training of nurses in every way possible. As the school expanded its curriculum, doctors lent their valuable time to take part in teaching students.[41] This was made possible by the sense of purpose shared by missionary doctors and nurses, founded on their faith and leading to a fruitful partnership. The student nurses thus received specialized training by highly qualified nurses and doctors. The doctors offered input regarding what was taught and how the student nurses were trained to meet the specific needs of the hospital. Dr. Holleman was an enthusiastic advocate for the nursing school, acting as the Hope Hospital superintendent for a period during the early twentieth century. In his retirement address to the hospital's board of directors, he mentioned the nurses' superior skills and indispensable service several times. He unequivocally affirmed their essential role: "The nurses are the very heart of any modern hospital. Doctor and patient are helpless without them."[42] This symbiotic relationship between doctor and nurses made full use of the abilities of both to meet the needs of the hospital while providing the student nurses with the best training possible.

In addition to the adoption of a dress code and rising educational expectations, the backgrounds of the students of the nursing school were another aspect of the school's evolution. In the beginning, before the school was accredited by the NAC, the school accepted just about anyone into the

---

40. Jessie Platz, interview by Julie Van Wyk, 23 June 1977, transcript, 22, The Old China Hands Oral History Project (1976–1977), H88-0113, Joint Archives of Holland.

41. Katherine R. Green, *Following the Great Physician: The Story of Our Medical Work in China*, printed pamphlet, n.d., 6, folder "Miscellaneous Publications, 1907–1970 (Amoy Mission)," China Mission Papers 1888–1979.

42. Clarence Holleman, "Address to the Board of Directors: Hope and Wilhelmina Hospital," 9 July 1941, 4, folder "Writings," Clarence H. Holleman Papers, W95-1196, Joint Archives of Holland.

program, with no consideration for age, sex, and academic qualifications.[43] This changed quickly in the first few years of the school's existence. Nienhuis, the founder, discovered that newly minted male nurses often moved on to train to be doctors rather than remain in the nursing profession. Thus, in 1927, the school admitted its last male student.[44] Nienhuis wanted to focus on women because of their perceived nurturing nature. She also learned early on that she must take only single women, for married women had far too little control over their own lives.[45] Veldman included in her account of the school one married female student abandoned by her husband "just before she was to graduate . . . [The husband] did return and said she must leave with him. She did not finish her training and she was the cause of the recent rule of only unmarried girls or widows being eligible."[46] Over time the school changed its guidelines on religion as well. At the beginning, it admitted only young Christians, but as time went on, that rule was revised to allow non-Christians to apply as well. One of the difficulties that the nursing school faced in its early years was the level of education required for those wishing to be admitted. This question of pre-qualification caused much difficulty because of the nursing profession's demand for well-educated individuals, although at the time the school was founded the profession was not yet respected in China. As Jessie Platz, one of the school's "trio" of missionary nurses, recalled in her retirement, "The high school principals would say, 'Oh, so and so doesn't do very well. Let's send her over to the nursing school,' instead of sending her on to senior high school."[47] Until nurses gradually gained respect in early twentieth-century China, the problem of the required entry qualification persisted.

As the population of students and staff grew, Hope and Wilhelmina Hospital saw the need for more housing. In 1932, plans to build a home for nurses were put in place. On April 1, 1933, the nurses' home was ready for occupancy.[48] Dr. Holleman was a big supporter not only of the nurses, but also of the idea of creating a home just for them. Before the building

43. Veldman, "History of the Hope Hospital School of Nursing," 6–6a.
44. Veldman, "History of the Hope Hospital School of Nursing," 11.
45. Veldman, "History of the Hope Hospital School of Nursing," 6.
46. Veldman, "History of the Hope Hospital School of Nursing," 6.
47. Platz, interview, transcript, 17.
48. Hope and Wilhelmina Hospital Printed Reports – 1933, 2–4, folder "Missions – Amoy (China) – Hope Hospital – Printed Reports, 1933–1949," Jeannette Veldman Papers.

of the nurses' home, they lived on the third floor of the hospital, but the facility had become too small. The creation of the nursing school pointed to the growing reliance of hospitals on nurses. The building of the nurses' home showed the increasing respect of the community for the nurses, for a great deal of the donations given for its construction came from the community. It is worth noting that the missionary nurses lived with their Chinese students. They did not separate themselves from the people that they were working with. This proximity allowed the missionary nurses to form relationships with their students in a way that would not have been possible otherwise.

Attending the nursing school opened many doors for Chinese young women, giving them an opportunity to shape their future. Graduates from Hope and Wilhelmina Hospital School of Nursing took different paths. Several young women decided to continue their education by going on to study midwifery at the hospital. Some were hired by the hospital as nurses and continued to work under Veldman, Nienhuis, and Platz. Others moved on to work in hospitals across the country. However, not every student continued in her nursing career. Some got married and subsequently left the profession to pursue life as mothers. More importantly, having a nursing degree gave the graduates more than just an employment opportunity; with the wider range of employment choices came a greater degree of control over their own lives. Nienhuis enclosed a description of the graduating class of 1937 with one of her letters, which gives one a picture of the career paths now available to these young Chinese women due to the training they had received at the nursing school. Six students graduated that year: Miss Koa, Miss Wu and her sister Miss Wu, Miss Khu, Miss Huang, and, finally, Miss Shao. Two stayed on to work at Hope and Wilhelmina Hospital, one accepted a position at a small country hospital, and one enrolled in a university in Nanjing for a public health degree.[49] Her sketch of each graduate brimmed with affection and pride, highlighting the progress that each young woman had made during her training, particularly in the areas of professional knowledge and Christian maturity.

The Christian faith was palpably present in the nursing school and permeated the ethos of patient care at the hospital. The nursing school initially admitted only Christians but later removed the restriction. This gave young Chinese women outside the Christian tradition an opportunity to

---

49. Jean Nienhuis to Gertrude Lieveuse, 21 July 1937, folder "Correspondence, 1921–1939," Jean Nienhuis Papers.

encounter Christianity as embodied by the missionary doctors and nurses and Chinese Christians in their day-to-day work in the hospital. Many of the young Christian nurses were very committed and saw a direct correlation between their work and their faith. Veldman told supporters back home of students praying and asking God to make them better Christians, and not simply better nurses.[50] Since nursing was closely associated with Christianity in its early days in China, people who entered the profession had an attitude of self-sacrifice in addition to professional aspirations. Many non-Christians did not understand the attraction that nursing held for young women because of the different principles that Christianity emphasized. The Xiamen community was particularly perplexed to see foreign women arrive to take care of their sick, with no concern for social status. The Chinese culture during that period could conceive that one should "care for your own sick of course, but to care for sick [people] not your own is slaves' work."[51] In contrast, Christian nurses considered it their godly duty to help those in need, without question or protest. One missionary nurse whose service in Xiamen was cut short by premature death, Helen Joldersma, wrote in her journal, "Oh, there is such satisfaction in being in the service of the King!"[52] Veldman echoed this sentiment in a letter to her family: "We do enjoy it. We do it because we love the Lord[,] because He wants us to serve Him by serving others."[53] To most of the missionary nurses' Chinese neighbors, experiencing joy and fulfillment through sacrificial service was a strange concept.

Hope and Wilhelmina Hospital School of Nursing in Times of Political Turmoil

Hope and Wilhelmina Hospital School of Nursing was not immune from the political turmoil that characterized China during the early twentieth century. Each new political development or armed conflict led to unique

50. Veldman to Friends, 6 September 1932.

51. Jeannette Veldman, interview by Greg Carlson and David M. Vander Haar, 30 June 1976, transcript, 15, The Old China Hands Oral History Project (1976–1977).

52. Tena Holkeboer, *Triumph of a Spirit: Glimpses from the Life of Helen Joldersma*, printed booklet (ca. 1931), 11, Helen Joldersma Papers, W11-1383, Joint Archives of Holland. Joldersma was an RCA medical missionary to China from 1926 to 1928, when she passed away at the age of 32 in China.

53. Jeannette Veldman to John Veldman, 21 June 1935, folder "Correspondence, 1935–1939," Jeannette Veldman Papers.

circumstances and new challenges for the nursing school and the hospital to cope with. The missionary nurses and their Chinese students all had to face an ever-changing political environment. The 1920s saw an upswing in both the Nationalist and Communist movements as they first collaborated briefly in a united front and then soon became bitter enemies.[54] Their struggle for power had a significant effect on the mission hospital, altering several aspects of the hospital's operation. Fighting between the Nationalist forces and the Communist rebels disrupted travel on some occasions, making it difficult for both patients and nurses to reach the hospital. By the late 1930s, conflict with Japan had escalated, leading to even more hardship for the hospital and nursing school. Travel was again affected and government operations such as the postal service were interrupted. Once the Japanese invaded Xiamen in May 1938, strict restrictions were placed on Chinese citizens and all Western nationals. These conflicts led to an increase in the number of hospital patients, as well as unease for the staff and students. Shifting ideological views caused tension in the hospital and the nursing school. Nationalist and Communist movements gave rise to anti-American sentiments among the locals. Communist propaganda led to distrust between the Chinese and Western staff, weakening their relationship. And war with Japan was the severest test the RCA's medical mission faced. The hospital staff and student nurses became relief workers in refugee camps.[55]

From the time Nienhuis started training student nurses in 1924 until Japanese forces took over the island of Gulangyu in 1941, Hope and Wilhelmina Hospital School of Nursing served the sick in Xiamen and its surrounding regions, as well as Chinese young women who aspired to become nurses. The student nurses were given strong female role models to emulate and befriend. By forming relationships built on trust, missionary nurses were able to get their pupils to go outside their comfort zones and push against traditional social boundaries and expectations. Thus, the missionaries gave their Chinese students a foundation to build themselves up as women and professionals in a changing society. Missionary nurses introduced their profession to China, even though their slowness in delegating upper-level professional positions to their Chinese colleagues may have hindered the full development of the profession in China. Nonetheless,

54. Spence, *The Search for Modern China*, 308–41.

55. Green, *"Following the Great Physician,"* 4. Please see the chapter "Faith and Humanitarian Aid in Wartime China, 1937–1941" by Claire Barrett for the RCA's relief work during the first four years of the Second Sino-Japanese War (1937–1945).

the overall impact of the missionary nurses' presence was beneficial. They broadened the opportunities available to young Chinese women. Student nurses received an invaluable education and acquired professional training and enduring life skills. Ultimately, those who received their medical training from missionaries recognized the significance of such training in their own lives and for the development of modern medicine in China.

The bombing of Pearl Harbor in 1941 drastically affected the missionaries who remained at Hope and Wilhelmina Hospital and on the island of Gulangyu. Japan's act of aggression against the United States and the latter's subsequent declaration of war meant that Western nationals in the international settlement on the island lost their legal privileges. The hospital and nursing school came under Japanese control, and the RCA missionaries on the island were subsequently repatriated. After the war, the RCA missionaries who returned to Gulangyu in 1946 noted that the hospital had been completely stripped. All equipment and supplies had been pilfered and the building left in disarray.[56] Not until the early summer of 1947 was Hope and Wilhelmina Hospital rehabilitated and reopened, with funds raised by Dr. Holleman from local and overseas Chinese and equipment and supplies acquired from various relief organizations.[57] Mission hospitals met a crucial need for medical services in war-torn China, but following the founding of the People's Republic of China in 1949 and the outbreak of the Korean War in 1950, harassment of missionaries by the new regime increased to the point that missionaries left China in great numbers. Fewer than 100 foreign Protestant missionaries remained in China by the spring of 1952, and the RCA's Amoy Mission came to an end in this exodus of Western missionaries.[58]

Bibliography

Primary Sources

China Mission Papers 1888-1979. W88-0315. Joint Archives of Holland, Holland, MI.
Clarence Holleman Papers. W95-1196. Joint Archives of Holland, Holland, MI.
Helen Joldersma Papers. W11-1383. Joint Archives of Holland, Holland, MI.
Jean Nienhuis Papers. W96-1208. Joint Archives of Holland, Holland, MI.

---

56. Henry De Pree and Ruth Broekema, "First Word from Kulangsu," *The Church Herald*, 22 February 1946.

57. De Jong, *The Reformed Church in China*, 309-10.

58. De Jong, *The Reformed Church in China*, 332.

Jeannette Veldman Papers. W89-1012. Joint Archives of Holland, Holland, MI.

MacGillivray, Donald. *A Century of Protestant Missions in China (1807-1907): Being the Centenary Conference Historical Volume.* Shanghai: American Presbyterian Mission Press, 1907.

The Old China Hands Oral History Project (1976-1977). H88-0113. Joint Archives of Holland, Holland, MI.

Secondary Sources

De Jong, Gerald F. *The Reformed Church in China, 1842-1951.* Historical Series of the Reformed Church in America 22. Grand Rapids: Eerdmans, 1992.

Group, Thetis M., and Joan I. Roberts. *Nursing, Physician Control, and the Medical Monopoly: Historical Perspectives on Gendered Inequality in Roles, Rights, and Range of Practice.* Bloomington: Indiana University Press, 2001.

Spence, Jonathan D. *The Search for Modern China.* 2nd ed. New York: Norton, 1999.

Watt, John. "Breaking into Public Service: The Development of Nursing in Modern China, 1870–1949." *Nursing History Review* 12 (2004) 67–96.

5

TENA HOLKEBOER

Single and Female in the China Mission of the Reformed Church in America, 1920-1948

GLORIA S. TSENG AND MADALYN DEJONGE

SEVERAL MONTHS AFTER GRADUATING from Hope College in 1920, Tena Holkeboer (1895-1965), born and raised in Holland, Michigan, left for her first term of service with the Amoy Mission of the Reformed Church in America (RCA). She would join the ranks of the 151 missionaries who served in the history of the Amoy Mission (1842-1950), among whom approximately eighty were women, and of this number, as many as thirty-one were single women. These single women's lengths of service ranged from two to fifty-three years. Holkeboer served in China for twenty-eight years. Of the single women missionaries who served for twenty-years or more—at least a dozen—one can reasonably assume that most, if not all, like Holkeboer, remained single all their lives.[1]

Women played a significant role in the great Protestant missionary movement of the nineteenth and early twentieth centuries. By the beginning

---

1. The Appendix of De Jong's *The Reformed Church in China* lists 151 missionaries, their dates of service in China, and the maiden names of its married female missionaries. Of this list, there are ten names whose gender is uncertain because they are uncommon or only initials are given.

of the last decade of the nineteenth century, women outnumbered men in the China mission field. Of the 1,296 missionaries representing forty-one Protestant missionary societies in China, there were 589 men, 391 wives, and 316 single women.[2] In contrast to the abundant scholarship on female monasticism in the history of Catholicism, the fact that many Protestant women missionaries were single and remained so for the duration of their missionary careers and beyond is an overlooked aspect of missionary history. Holkeboer's long missionary career offers a glimpse into the experiences of single female missionaries and their contribution to the Protestant missionary movement.

In Holkeboer, one sees an accomplished woman of great ability, deep piety, indomitable spirit, and a tender heart. She was a well-known and respected missionary in RCA circles in her era, featured in *The Intelligencer-Leader*, the denomination's periodical, and in biographical fliers distributed by the denomination's Board of Foreign Missions and Woman's Board of Foreign Missions.[3] In Holkeboer's missionary career, one sees that singleness both liberated a woman to achieve remarkable accomplishments in the mission field and exacerbated the loneliness caused by prolonged separation from one's family of origin. She was part of a close-knit missionary community in China and deeply devoted to the people whom she served, but all her letters home—they were numerous and lengthy—repeatedly spoke of her longing for her family and revealed an unflagging interest in the details of home life, and the interest continued and even grew as her siblings married and had children of their own. Holkeboer's story may or may not be representative, but it lifts the veil, ever so slightly, over the experiences of single Protestant women in faraway mission fields.

When Tena Holkeboer left for China on September 25, 1920, as a new missionary commissioned by the Woman's Board of Foreign Missions of the RCA to the denomination's Amoy Mission, she was a young, single woman of twenty-five, the oldest of eight siblings from a tightly-knit and pious Dutch-American family of modest means. A graduate of Hope Preparatory School, she had taught for several years at Holland Christian School prior to enrolling at Hope College in preparation to become a missionary. Her

2. Latourette, *A History of Christian Missions in China*, 406.

3. Cover of *The Intelligencer-Leader*, March 27, 1942; Woman's Board of Foreign Missions, Reformed Church in America, "Tena Holkeboer, Teacher and Evangelist in China," July 1942; and Board of Foreign Missions, Reformed Church in America, "Tena Holkeboer," April 1948, folder "Biographical Information, 1942–1965," Tena Holkeboer Papers, W88–0055, Joint Archives of Holland, Holland, MI.

father had passed away suddenly while she was in college.⁴ Now she was leaving her widowed mother and seven younger siblings. At this point, one had no way of foreseeing that this was the beginning of a long and fruitful missionary career, and of the responsibilities that she would come to assume and the lives she would touch in the decades to come.

For now, all was new to this young missionary recruit and her colleague, Jean Nienhuis, also a brand-new, single female missionary,⁵ who was eight years Holkeboer's senior and from the same hometown, and with whom she would develop a close lifelong friendship. Aboard the ship to China, she saw Chinese up close for the first time—fellow passengers, but in steerage, not first class, where she and her fellow missionaries were; and workers on the ship, including waiters who served them at table during mealtimes. In her first letter home from her first ocean voyage to China—twelve pages written across five days—Holkeboer showed herself a keen and sympathetic observer in her description of the steerage passengers: "There are only men, as far as I can see, they are all Chinese. They surely are a very rough set & keep themselves busy with smoking & gambling largely. I saw their sleeping quarters the day before the boat sailed. They're all herded together in one large room in which there are rows of what are supposed to be beds."⁶ Of the Chinese workers, she said, "With the exception of the officers all the employees on this boat are Chinese. I never saw such willing, hard-working people. The same men keep cabins clean, answer bells, and wait tables. One of them told Mr. Harrison that they worked from 4:30 A.M. until 11 P.M. It seems cruel . . ."⁷ She witnessed a touching scene one evening. An elderly woman who had trouble walking was struggling to get over a step between the deck and the interior of the ship with the help of another woman. Then "[t]he deck steward (a Chinaman) saw their difficulty & stepped up & took her arm & helped her in just as tenderly as tho it

---

4. Woman's Board of Foreign Missions, Reformed Church in America, "Tena Holkeboer, Teacher and Evangelist in China," July 1942; Board of Foreign Missions, Reformed Church in America, "Tena Holkeboer," April 1948; donor's note accompanying the Holkeboer collection, folder "Biographical Information, 1942–1965."

5. Jean Nienhuis is one of the three missionary nurses featured in the chapter "Hope and Wilhelmina Hospital School of Nursing: The Role of Missionary Nurses in Xiamen, China," by Katelyn Dickerson, in this volume.

6. Tena Holkeboer to Dear, dear mother, brothers, & sisters, 27 September 1920, folder "Correspondence, 1920–1972, n.d.," Tena Holkeboer Papers. The letters by Holkeboer used in this chapter are all from this collection.

7. Tena Holkeboer to Dear, dear mother, brothers, & sisters, 27 September 1920.

was his own mother."[8] These first impressions led the young Holkeboer to conclude, "I'm going to like the Chinese people, I am sure, if they're at all like those we have on board. They seem to be so sympathetic, so willing to help, & so eager to learn."[9]

Since the training Holkeboer received in college did not include language study, her assumptions about the Chinese of Xiamen on her first journey to China were based on observations on the ship, a little prior knowledge, and some preconceived notions. Before traveling to the Far East, her whole world was Holland, Michigan, with no exposure to Chinese people and few opportunities to learn about Chinese culture. Fortunately, her first two years in the field would be devoted to filling these gaps in her knowledge. Before ministering to the people, she would have the opportunity to explore China and undertake an intensive study of written Chinese and the Min dialect, spoken in southern Fujian province, where the Amoy Mission was located. Because she had a natural curiosity and a remarkable talent for learning languages, within a year of arriving in the field she went from observing the local people and believing that she would like them to conversing with them and developing relationships with them.[10]

On November 15, 1920, Holkeboer arrived at the RCA's Amoy Mission, based in the international settlement on the small island of Gulangyu and with stations and outstations in the city of Xiamen, an island of about fifty-one square miles, and up-country on the mainland. Holkeboer embraced the busy life of a missionary wholeheartedly. She enthusiastically described her weekday schedule in a letter to her family in response to her brother Peter's inquiry:

> I get up at 6:30, at 7:00 we have 15 minutes of intercessory prayer together, 7:15 is breakfast, 7:45 prayer & Bible reading with Chinese servants, 8:00–10:00 language study. 10:00–12:30 teaching, 12:30–1:00 dinner, 1:00–2:00 quiet hour, 2:00–3:30 study, 3:30–4:20 teach singing, 4:30 tea, 5:00–6:00 exercise, shopping, 7:15 supper, & after that usually study or letters or preparation for classes.[11]

---

8. Tena Holkeboer to Dear, dear mother, brothers, & sisters, 27 September 1920.

9. Tena Holkeboer to Dear, dear mother, brothers, & sisters, 27 September 1920.

10. Tena Holkeboer to Dear mamma, brothers & sisters, 12 December 1920; Tena Holkeboer to Dear All, 21 March 1921; Tena Holkeboer to Dear Folks at Home, 18 October 1921.

11. Tena Holkeboer to Dear mamma, brothers, & sisters, 9 January 1921.

She began teaching at the RCA's school for girls on the island of Gulangyu from the start of her time in China. Teaching and later school administration would be her primary responsibility as a missionary. She also eagerly took on the challenge of language study. In just nine months after her arrival in China, she successfully passed her first year's language examination,[12] which was no easy task. As Holkeboer explained in a general letter to relatives, "For the first year I must read & translate 4 books in the printed language, learn to read and write 600 of these characters, be able to talk 10 minutes in Chinese, and write an essay in [romanized] Chinese."[13]

In the depth of her heart, Holkeboer was an evangelist. She seized every available opportunity to help with the work of churches in Amoy, visit Chinese homes with experienced missionaries, and go to the mission's up-country stations—Tong'an, Xiaoxi, and Zhangzhou[14]—even before she was conversant in Chinese. Her fervor is readily evident in one of her earliest letters home:

> I *love* to go into these homes & come into personal touch with the people... Oh, to see these heathen women *drink in*, as it were, every word you say, to see their eagerness to listen, and to know that there is a message for these thirsting souls, is such an inspiration to me that I *long* to get to the stage where I, too, can speak to them![15]

About half a year after her arrival in China, Holkeboer could tell her family back in Holland, Michigan, that she was able to understand Chinese conversation "fairly well" if people were not speaking too fast. In fact, she had just heard a sermon in Chinese, which she had understood "almost entirely."[16] She was eager to enter fully into the work of the mission field. She took on more teaching at the girls' schools and began joining fellow missionary William Vander Meer on Sunday afternoons to organize a Sunday School for Zhushujiao church in Xiamen.[17] Classes were to be organized "for old and young," the purpose of which was "to have the church

---

12. Tena Holkeboer to Dear, dear folks at home, 6 June 1921.
13. Tena Holkeboer to Dear relatives, 9 March 1921.
14. Formerly Tong-an, Sio-khe, and Chiang-chiu respectively.
15. Tena Holkeboer to Dear ones at home, 12 January 1921.
16. Tena Holkeboer to Dear All, 21 March 1921.
17. Referred to as Tek-chhiu-kha ("under bamboo trees" in the local dialect) in missionary correspondence. Tena Holkeboer to Dear Mamma, brothers, & sisters, 18 April 1921.

members bring in heathen neighbors & friends."[18] Holkeboer turned out to be an indispensable coworker, for as a man in a society where men and women had little contact with the opposite sex outside one's family, Vander Meer could "do nothing for the women's & girls' part of the work" on his own.[19]

Holkeboer went about this work with gusto and established a rudimentary system for teaching a group of women and girls totally unaccustomed to formal schooling. She separated the women into four classes: one for those who could read and study the Bible, one for those who were learning to read, and one for those who were too old to learn to read and were being taught to commit hymns and texts to memory, and one for those who were new to church.[20] The work required both determination and flexibility, both of which Holkeboer exhibited. She said with some satisfaction to her family, "You can't imagine what it means to get system into such work, the women are all ignorant & can't see any reason why you should do things that way & so you've got to keep your eyes open all the time & steer each one into the right section & keep them there... they come in at all times, you know—many don't know the use of a clock."[21] Her labors soon began to bear fruit, as in the transformation of a "heathen" woman who once burst into her Sunday School; it was the woman's first time to church and only a few weeks after Holkeboer had introduced her teaching system at the church:

> She came in, her face beaming, & shouted so you could hear her thruout the church, "I've come, here I am!" Seeing a friend she called out to her & greeted her just as noisily. I went up to her & asked her whether she wished to hear or learn to read. She proudly displayed a hymn book & shouted out about that. By that time everybody was watching her & those who knew better smiled. Finally I got her sitting next to her friend & didn't try to do any more for her for that day except to tell her to come again.[22]

This woman continued to attend Sunday School and began learning to read in the months that followed. By the end of 1921, Holkeboer was spending Sundays all day in Xiamen, visiting her Sunday School students in their

18. Tena Holkeboer to Dear All, 21 March 1921.
19. Tena Holkeboer to Dear All, 21 March 1921.
20. Holkeboer to Dear Mamma, brothers, & sisters, 18 April 1921.
21. Holkeboer to Dear Mamma, brothers, & sisters, 18 April 1921.
22. Holkeboer to Dear Mamma, brothers, & sisters, 18 April 1921.

homes after church to answer questions they had from the catechism book, and she went home with this woman one Sunday afternoon in December. She gave a moving account of this visit in a letter to her family in America:

> ... I told her I was going home with her. You should have seen her face light up! So I followed the old body thru the narrow dirty streets to her little 4x5 room which was just big enough to hold her short narrow bed of boards & a tiny round stool.... We took the catechism & I tried to explain to her who God was. She had already grasped that idea fairly well & so we went on to Christ & His work. This was wholly incomprehensible to her, & I left the book right there, explained first the need of a Savior & then told His life upon earth. I became so full of it that I forgot I was talking Chinese, & I talked straight on for nearly an hour. I just felt inspired. And as for the woman, she just seemed to *drink* it in. When I told of Christ's suffering and death the tears trickled down her cheeks. Oh, what joy I had in telling that story for the first time to one who had *never* heard it before! And now that I have once gone out alone & find that I have enough of a vocabulary so that people can understand me, I shall hope to begin to do regular personal work... God grant that this poor old body may find the light dawning more & more upon her soul, & that she may accept the salvation which is in Christ Jesus![23]

Holkeboer's first two years of service in China were filled with new experiences, both joys and challenges. She and Nienhuis joined a close-knit missionary community on Gulangyu, who warmly welcomed them into their ranks. The two single women missionaries spent their holidays in China in the company of fellow missionaries. New Year's Day 1921 was spent with Frederick and Bata Weersing and William Vander Meer, the latter also a new missionary who went to China the same year as Holkeboer and Nienhuis:

> In the morning we received Chinese guests who came to wish us a happy new year. In the afternoon we went with the Weersings & Bill Vander Meer to visit a famous temple on the Amoy side. We took a boat over to this place & after seeing the temple went back to the beach & had a *weenie roast*! Came back by star light. I never *dreamed* of doing such a thing over here. Had a lovely time.[24]

---

23. Tena Holkeboer to Dear Ones at Home, 12 December 1921.
24. Tena Holkeboer to Dear ones at home, 3 January 1921.

The small island of Gulangyu gave Holkeboer and Nienhuis their first experience of bathing in the ocean and going on boat rides, as the beach was within walking distance from missionary residences. It was the Boots and the Beltmans—the latter also new missionaries and had been on the same steamer to China as Holkeboer and Nienhuis—who introduced them to these activities. Holkeboer cheerfully recounted their evening outings during a week in June 1921 to her family: "Isn't that going some? We have never gone boat riding, nor bathing before & here everything was packed into one week—it never rains but it pours! Doesn't sound much like what you expect a missionary's life to be, eh? More like a resorter!"[25]

There were, however, real challenges to the missionary's life and health. Winters were mild in Fujian province compared to Michigan. Nonetheless, indoor temperatures dropped to the 50s Fahrenheit without heating. Holkeboer learned to live without a fire her first winter in China: "I am wearing my heavy underclothing, my warm sailor dress & my sweater on top of that but, after sitting still for a time my hands & feet are numb with cold. The Sanloh[26] ladies have gotten used to doing without fires & so we are learning too, to do without them. Oh, for a furnace!"[27] The return of warm weather meant continual rain and dampness, and their companions: mold, mosquitoes, fleas, rats, cockroaches, centipedes, and the like.[28] Discomfort turned into real health threats in summer, when contagious diseases abounded. After a long and damp spring, an outbreak of plague and cholera in Xiamen and some of the up-country regions in the summer of 1922 ravaged the population: "Whole families are just wiped out in a few days' time. . . . sometimes death comes inside of a few hours. In a kindergarten belonging to one of our Amoy churches, 5 little children died in one week. . . . The death-rate these days is appalling."[29] The threat of plague was such that missionaries temporarily stopped making home visits.[30]

To escape the worst of the summer heat, many missionaries went up to the mountains in July and August. Holkeboer and Nienhuis were both

---

25. Tena Holkeboer to Dear all, 20 June 1921.

26. The missionary residence on Gulangyu where Holkeboer lived at this time, known as 三落姑娘楼 (sanluo gu'niang lou) to local Chinese.

27. Holkeboer to Dear ones at home, 3 January 1921.

28. Tena Holkeboer to Dear, dear ones at home, 9 May 1921; Tena Holkeboer to Dear, dear all, 16 May 1921.

29. Tena Holkeboer to Dear All, 12 June 1922.

30. Tena Holkeboer to Dear All, 12 June 1922.

introduced to this summer migration during their first summer in China, when they went to Da Mao Mountain[31] with Leona Vander Linden, another single female missionary who first arrived in the mission field in 1909. Holkeboer's first impressions were relief from the debilitating heat of the plains and awe at the beauty of the scenery:

> Yes, we're on the mountain top at last, 1800 ft. above sea-level. Oh, what a relief to get away from the heat of the plains!...The scenery here is magnificent—we are hemmed in by mountains on every side.... From some of the peaks we get a wonderful view—beyond the mountains with the little villages nestling here & there in the valleys there is the deep blue ocean with its mountainous islands— Amoy & Kolongsu are plainly visible.[32]

The three single women missionaries spent the entire summer of 1921, from late July to early September, on Da Mao Mountain in frequent fellowship with other missionaries—those of their own mission and those from an English mission with which the Amoy Mission had good relations. As the time to return to Gulangyu approached, Holkeboer could say, "I certainly have had a happy summer, but I am looking forward now to taking a more active part in the work."[33]

In fact, from the time of her arrival in China, Holkeboer stretched herself to take "a more active part in the work." She did so by learning the language, by participating in the evangelistic outreach and congregational work of the mission's Chinese churches, and by teaching in the mission's schools for girls, her main responsibility as a missionary of the Amoy Mission. More importantly, she stepped far beyond her comfort zone to make herself a more effective missionary. She approached eating Chinese food as seriously as she would any missionary task: "I can't get used to Chinese food. I eat it when opportunity offers because I am determined to be one with them but it's hard work."[34] And she meant what she said. When her first school year in China drew to a close in June 1921, the eighth-grade graduating class gave a feast, which fellow missionary Lilly Duryee, the then principal, and Holkeboer attended. Holkeboer's feisty spirit and

---

31. Known to the missionaries as Toa-bo Soan, or Big Hat Mountain, in the Minnan dialect.
32. Tena Holkeboer to Dear, dear folks at home, 18 July 1921.
33. Tena Holkeboer to Dear, dear folks at home, 29 August 1921.
34. Tena Holkeboer to Dear Mamma, brothers, & sisters, 25 April 1921.

determination to make herself one among the local people were evident in her effort to eat a morsel of everything that was presented:

> It's a good thing I feel so well or I never could stand Chinese food in this hot weather. But I ate something of whatever came along tho some things still make me shiver inside. One thing which I had never seen before was buried eggs. They take eggs and bury them for *months* until they are entirely black inside. These they consider a very great delicacy... Miss Duryee said I had better not take any (she refused it herself), but I determined to take it if for no other reason than to say I had eaten buried eggs![35]

And when her second school year began in September 1921, Holkeboer, fresh from the summer spent on Da Mao Mountain, took the bold step of teaching a Bible class in Chinese, in addition to the subjects she taught during her first year:

> I begin at once to-day teaching English & music, & next week I'm going to start teaching one class in Chinese. We are to study the book of Acts from a text book. I'll make a great many blunders of course, but it's the best way to learn & I've just *dared*. I asked to have this class, for I'm eager to get into some of the work for which I came out & I know I'll learn to talk a great deal faster that way.[36]

Ever desirous to push herself to master the language, Holkeboer also took on morning prayer, which was conducted in Chinese, with the students in the lower grades twice a week. This, too, required courage: "Tho I long to get into it, I dread to get started. It will take quite a bit of preparation at first because my vocabulary is still so very limited, so I thot twice a week was enough. Then when I get a bit used to it I can take it oftener."[37] These efforts bore fruit—Holkeboer passed the first half of the second-year language exam in early November that year, only one year from the week she started studying the language.[38]

After two years on Gulangyu, Holkeboer was transferred to the up-country station of Tong'an. In many ways, the assignment at the Tong'an station, some twenty miles inland north of Xiamen island and accessible by Xixi Brook, gave Holkeboer the opportunity to immerse herself in "the

---

35. Tena Holkeboer to Dear Folks at Home, 25 June 1921.
36. Tena Holkeboer to Dear Folks at Home, 12 September 1921.
37. Tena Holkeboer to Dear, dear ones at home, 18 September 1921.
38. Tena Holkeboer to Dear, dear folks at home, 7 November 1921.

work" for which she went to China. Tong'an was familiar to her, as she had already visited the station a few times, and she had high regard for Dr. and Mrs. Vandeweg, who were responsible for the RCA hospital there.[39] As she looked forward to her future work in China atop Big Hat Mountain at the beginning of September 1921, she told her family in Michigan,

> As for me, for this year I'll surely be in Amoy. As for the future, it's not at all certain. One faction declares I shall always be kept here in the main station, while another is bound that I shall go up to Tong-an next year. Time will tell! Personally I should prefer the up-country work for I can more easily get into personal touch with the people there, but I shall be happy to work wherever I am most needed, wherever God can use me best for the advancement of His kingdom.[40]

Field assignments in the Amoy Mission were made collectively by the missionaries themselves. Every summer, all missionaries of the Amoy Mission gathered together for about a week to discuss matters of concern to the mission and work allocations for the coming year, hence Holkeboer's uncertainty at the time.[41] The decision to send Holkeboer to the Tong'an station was made in the mission meeting of 1922, and, due to various personnel considerations and the personal desires of some of the missionaries, it took four or five rounds of voting to reach the required two-thirds majority regarding Holkeboer's assignment.[42] It was understood to be a temporary assignment:

> It was proposed that I remain a member of the Amoy district with a view to working in the schools here, but that for the next school year of 10 months, I be *loaned* to the Tong-an district so that Miss Zwemer might have a companion, the Tong-an schools for girls & women a chance to get on their feet with 2 workers in charge, & I also have the privilege of at least that much up-country experience.[43]

---

39. Tena Holkeboer to Dear ones at home, 12 January 1921; Tena Holkeboer to Dear, dear all, 30 May 1921; Tena Holkeboer to Dear, dear folks at home, 3 January 1922.

40. Tena Holkeboer to Dear ones at home, 6 September 1921.

41. Tena Holkeboer to Dear Folks at Home, 25 June 1921; Tena Holkeboer to Dear Ones at Home, 5 July 1921; Tena Holkeboer to Dear, dear folks at home, 13 July 1921.

42. Tena Holkeboer to Dear, dear All, 30 June 1922; Tena Holkeboer to Dear, dear all, 6 July 1922; Tena Holkeboer to Dear, dear home folks, 11 July 1922.

43. Holkeboer to Dear, dear home folks, 11 July 1922.

Unbeknownst to her at the time, Holkeboer would remain at the Tong'an station until her first furlough in the summer of 1925—three challenging and satisfying years in her life as a young missionary.

In September 1922, after a second summer on Da Mao Mountain, Holkeboer set off for Tong'an with both keen anticipation and much trepidation, as veteran missionary Nellie Zwemer, with whom she was to work, was to arrive later from furlough in America: "I dread going up & opening schools, starting work with everything new & strange,—if only she were here now & we could start in together!" Although her primary responsibility was teaching at the girls' and women's schools, Holkeboer also assisted at the station hospital often. What she saw and observed during her first month in Tong'an overwhelmed her: "Experiences crowd upon one another so thick & fast here that the one crowds out the former one before I have time to write about it! . . . The sights I see at the hospital every day are simply indescribable."[44] These included a young mother with an enormous abscess on her hip, a baby boy whose throat and chin were swollen and rotten from an infection, and numerous babies covered in boils and sores—sights that led her to exclaim, "Oh, the cruelties of heathenism!!"[45] As students of the girls' and women's schools arrived from their villages near and far in the days leading up to the beginning of the school year, they bared their hearts to Holkeboer: "Pupils. . . all come in to talk things over, sometimes with a Bible woman, sometimes with a preacher, sometimes with parents. And nearly every one has some tale of woe to tell, so much so that one gets *heart-sick* from all the misery one hears about."[46] Even so, Holkeboer soon grew to love her work at the Tong'an station despite illnesses, wartime unrest, and the death of fellow missionary Dr. Vandeweg. At the beginning of her first school year in Tong'an, Holkeboer had an attack of malaria, when she "passed thru some days of real misery."[47] More serious was a long bout with dengue fever lasting more than four weeks toward the end of 1922, when she went back to Gulangyu to visit Jean Nienhuis.[48] It was during this long period of Holkeboer's illness and confinement on Gulangyu when

---

44. Tena Holkeboer to Dear Loved Ones at home, 2 October 1922.
45. Tena Holkeboer to Dear Loved Ones at home, 2 October 1922.
46. Tena Holkeboer to Dear, dear ones at home, 9 October 1922.
47. Tena Holkeboer to Dear, dear folks at home, 27 October 1922.
48. Tena Holkeboer to Dear, dear folks at home, 24 November 1922; Tena Holkeboer to Dear loved ones at home, 4 December 1922; Tena Holkeboer to Dear, dear sister mine, 13 December 1922.

Dr. Vandeweg fell ill and passed away suddenly in Tong'an and she became a loyal friend to Mrs. Vandeweg.[49] And the backdrop to all this was the political fragmentation of China and the general lawless conditions of the warlord period:

> The region roundabout is still very much unsettled. There are constant rumors of war & bandits, and certain parts do suffer a great deal. Just at present the southern forces are in control again, but they say the northern soldiers are preparing for battle near Chiang-chiu[50] & our missionaries may have to come down from there for safety. Everything is uncertain. There are British, American, & Japanese war vessels in the harbor here all the time for the protection of foreign interests.[51]

An often-repeated refrain in the letters from Holkeboer's first year in Tong'an was "tired but happy" after a full day's work. Holkeboer especially enjoyed visiting the mission's outstations and the homes of Chinese believers and unbelievers in surrounding villages, sometimes with Zwemer, who was in her early sixties, and sometimes on her own. Two letters from January 1923 tell of such visits:

> Yesterday we went together to one of the out-stations between 5 & 6 miles away. Miss Z. preached in the A.M., and in the P.M. I actually took charge of the whole service. Tho I have given a good many little talks by this time, this was the first time I did anything like this. We had one chair[52] between us so that I walked about 2/3 of the way. This, together with the service, resulted in a pretty tired girl at night, but she was as happy as she was tired, so it didn't matter. Oh, it is such joy to bring the message of life to those who are so needy![53]

And two weeks later,

> Sunday I went out to our nearest out-station, about 2 ½ miles away. Miss Zwemer was asked to take the morning service at the chapel there but was too tired so that she couldn't walk it, and

---

49. Holkeboer to Dear, dear folks at home, 24 November 1922; Holkeboer to Dear loved ones at home, 4 December 1922.

50. Zhangzhou in modern pinyin.

51. Holkeboer to Dear, dear folks at home, 24 November 1922.

52. Referring to a sedan chair, carried on poles by two or more hired men, the most common means of land transportation in that era.

53. Tena Holkeboer to Dear, dear folks at home, 8 January 1923.

because it was a "lucky day" for brides, she couldn't hire a single chair in the city! So I went to take her place—not that I could *fill* her place, but I did the best I could. It still is quite an effort for me to do this kind of thing, even tho I don't prepare a new talk each time, but I enjoy it very much & always return from such a day's work tired but happy.[54]

In Zwemer, who was also a single woman missionary, Holkeboer had a kindred spirit and congenial companion. In the mission meeting of July 1923, it was decided that Holkeboer would stay on in Tong'an until her furlough, for Zwemer was having some health trouble. Holkeboer was glad for this decision for several reasons, among which were her love for the work and her appreciation for Zwemer's companionship:

> It surely is a relief to me to know that I don't have to move again... Now I can go back and feel that the foundation is laid & I'm ready to build on it. I have learned to *love* the work & the workers, the Christians in the various out-stations, & my little school-girls, and I am indeed thankful that I may go back to them in the fall. It is also a great privilege that I can keep on working with Miss Zwemer, for our aims & ideals & sympathies are *one*, & no one can realize quite what that means until they have experienced living far away from home & congenial surroundings.[55]

Overall, Holkeboer's years in Tong'an appear to have been deeply satisfying, even though very few of her letters from the subsequent two years remain.

In 1925, at the age of thirty, Holkeboer completed her first term of service. Furloughs were usually one year in length, but because of illness, her return to China was delayed from 1926 to 1927, during which time she also earned an M.A. from Columbia University.[56] She rejoined the girls' school on the island of Gulangyu, where she had first started out as a new missionary. In a letter, she told a friend that the 1927–1928 school year had been "a year rich in blessing and in the assurance of God's presence and His power."[57] For the twenty-seven girls who accepted Christ and the fifty who requested to prepare for church membership, and for the Christian students who were stirred to renewed commitment during this first year of

---

54. Tena Holkeboer to Dear home folks, 24 January 1923.

55. Tena Holkeboer to Dear folks at home, 10 July 1923.

56. Woman's Board of Foreign Missions, "Tena Holkeboer, Teacher and Evangelist in China."

57. Tena Holkeboer to Dora, 7 August 1928.

her second term, her heart overflowed with praise—"I can say from a full heart: 'Praise God from Whom all blessings flow!'"[58] And now, a seasoned missionary, she was appointed principal of the school beginning the following academic year, a testimony to her abilities as an educator and a leader. Holkeboer knew that it would be a heavy responsibility, with difficulties involved and great potential for spiritual influence: "It will be especially difficult because our Chinese head-teacher has also resigned, and for the present I must carry the double load as we can get no one suitable to take his place. Pray for me that God may *enable* me. I *believe* He has placed me here, and I trust Him for my every need. Oh, I *long* to see the school a real spiritual power in the lives of the girls and for the work of the Kingdom in this portion of the great Harvest field."[59]

Holkeboer's first year as principal was possibly her greatest challenge as a missionary yet. The girls' middle school on Gulangyu had many more pupils than the girls' and women's schools in Tong'an. There were twenty-four and twenty-six graduates from the senior high and junior high graduating classes of 1929 respectively.[60] Holkeboer had reason to be proud of her graduates. She said to her family that all the senior graduates were Christians, many of whom were "very earnest Christians" desiring to "give their lives to Christian work."[61] Nursing, college, Bible training, and teaching in mission schools were among their goals after graduation. She had high hopes for this class, whom she taught in a Bible course in their final year: "Oh, if they will go back & witness in the inland places for Him, then all the heartaches, all the anxieties & tears will have been more than worthwhile!"[62] A month later, when she was vacationing in the Philippines with Jean Nienhuis and another single woman missionary, Elizabeth Bruce, she reflected on this first year in the principalship: "I had been literally buried in my work, and all other thots and feelings were shut out. . . . I've been under a tremendous nervous strain. . ."[63] Time away on the mountains in the Philippines restored her good cheer, and she expressed to her family her gratitude to God and faith in His ways: "God's ways are indeed unexpected, for little did I dream it would be my privilege to see so much of the world.

58. Tena Holkeboer to Dora, 7 August 1928.
59. Tena Holkeboer to Dora, 7 August 1928.
60. Tena Holkeboer to My precious family, 30 June 1929.
61. Tena Holkeboer to My precious family, 30 June 1929.
62. Tena Holkeboer to My precious family, 30 June 1929.
63. Tena Holkeboer to My own precious family, 23 July 1929.

Nor has it been anything I have ever especially craved, but as it is I can only thank Him humbly & pray that God may help me to use my privileges aright."[64]

During her second term, Holkeboer was much busier than during her first term, and she no longer kept up a strict schedule of weekly letters home. In many ways, she went beyond the call of duty in her work. As her second school year as principal began, she invited the school's teachers to her home. She and the teachers discussed the school's problems, had dinner, and a social time afterwards. She was hopeful for the new school year: "So the spirit of coöperation should be better than last year ... Oh pray that God may use me here to make this school truly a training school for sending out graduates filled with the desire to bring their fellow men in touch with Christ!"[65] Before the end of the first semester of the 1929-30 academic year, she moved into the student dormitory, even though it meant giving up time that she could have entirely to herself: "Sometimes it seems a big price to pay to be living here, for from morning to night there is little or no time definitely my own, but on the other hand, I feel I have gained a great deal in learning to know the girls better. And they understand me better. More and more they are opening up and responding in a way they never did before."[66] In addition, Holkeboer was assuming more mission-wide responsibilities. She was traveling more—three sea voyages from July 1929 to January 1930: "Am getting to be quite a seasoned traveller—my third sea trip within six months—to Manila in July, to Hongkong in October, & now north to Shanghai! 'A privileged person,' I hear you say. Yes, indeed..."[67] And she now sat on many committees, adding to her leadership responsibilities in the mission: "If I only could get some rest... But there's no *question* of that at least until after the deputation is gone. They are to be here from Mar 15th to April 15th. During that time we are to have a week of Mission meeting, and our school is to celebrate its *10th* anniversary. It means a memorial service, a concert, and a pageant.... Then they've been putting me on so many committees[,] three of which meet this week—and that means hours of time ... I'll be in the midst of a strenuous time ... and ask you especially to pray for me."[68]

64. Tena Holkeboer to My own precious family, 23 July 1929.
65. Tena Holkeboer to My own precious home-folks, 7 October 1929.
66. Tena Holkeboer to My own precious family, 4 December [1929].
67. Tena Holkeboer to My own dear home-folks, 31 January 1930.
68. Tena Holkeboer to My own dear home-folks, 24 February 1930.

One significant and formative experience for Holkeboer during the first half of her second term in China[69] was the discovery of a cyst or tumor in her abdomen that required surgery sometime toward the end of the 1929–30 school year. Her letter to her family from June 1930 referred to it as a recurrence of her "old trouble," which leads one to surmise that it might have been connected to the health issue that had prolonged her first furlough.[70] Be that as it may, at the time of her writing, the mission's doctors—Edward Strick, Clarence Holleman, and Richard Hofstra—believed that an operation should be performed as soon as possible, and Holkeboer was weighing her options, whether to have it done in the mission's own hospital on Gulangyu or elsewhere in China:

> I prefer to have it done here—I just *hate* to travel when I'm physically below par, but the doctors here hate to operate on a fellow missionary. As Dick says, "It's like operating on one of your own family." If it's done here Strick will be chief surgeon & Holleman & Dick will assist. Jean is the only nurse, and my staying here would be very hard on her. She's much stronger than last year, but I hate to put the extra load on her.[71]

Late one night a month after she first broke the news of the tumor to her family, she wrote a long, heartfelt letter to give a detailed account of the discovery of the tumor and its miraculous disappearance.[72] Following the mission meeting that took place in the spring of that year, she came down with a severe attack of colitis and began to suffer constant and severe pain. One night she discovered a large, hard lump on her right side after awaking from pain and trying to locate its source. Then came the diagnosis by Dr. Holleman, which was confirmed by Dr. Strick—a mass that was the size of two big oranges—and the recommended treatment of immediate operation. Holkeboer, however, wanted to finish the school term first. Acknowledging her spiritual struggles during this time of illness and fear, the letter recounts a turning point that occurred about three weeks before the school term ended:

---

69. Only one letter survives from 1933 and none from 1934; thus, a big part of her second term must remain unknown.

70. Tena Holkeboer to My own precious family, 7 June 1930.

71. Tena Holkeboer to My own precious family, 7 June 1930. See also Tena Holkeboer to My own dear family, 20 June 1930.

72. Tena Holkeboer to My own precious mother, brothers, and sisters, 9 July 1930.

> One night I had a long battle, but it ended in victory. I cannot tell you more, except that in that hour when I realized that God had conquered and was working out His will in me, I was given faith to believe that if it were *best* for me, He could remove my trouble miraculously, as sure as our Lord did it for men when upon earth. I did not ask that it be removed—I was just as willing then to go thru pain and suffering and whatever else it might mean, as to be healed from it. My prayer was simply, "Lord, if Thou *wilt*, Thou *canst*." If it were not His best will for me, I did not want healing. And I left matters there, having absolute peace—*all dread* was removed.[73]

Four days later, Holkeboer remembered the doctors' order to watch the growth closely, and upon examining the area of the growth, she could not find it. At first, she could not believe that the growth was no longer there: "I did not *dare* to think God had actually taken it away, so I waited a few days, and then told Jean. She too, was unable to find it."[74] A few more days passed before Holkeboer told Dr. Holleman, who did not believe her. Two more weeks passed, and when Dr. Holleman examined her in preparation for the operation, he could find nothing. Holkeboer's description of Holleman's reaction, who blamed himself for a misdiagnosis, is touching: "Dr. H was simply *baffled*. He was glad he had Strick's verdict as well as his own. He called himself a second-rate doctor for making such a blunder, but in reality he had taken *every possible* precaution and made all his examinations very thoroughly. Dr. Hofstra is here too now, and all three doctors are pondering at what may have happened."[75] The spiritual significance of this experience was clear to Holkeboer: "It is hard to desist from seeking a natural explanation for it all . . . But in this case I can attribute my recovery to nothing except God's wonder-working power—in response to faith . . . God is indeed *my* Heavenly Father, responding to the need of His child."[76] Her miraculous recovery must have also greatly encouraged many in this tightly-knit mission: "Folks here have been just lovely during these weeks of suspense, and I learned after all was settled that without my knowing it, several had been praying that God might remove the trouble without

---

73. Tena Holkeboer to My own precious mother, brothers, and sisters, 9 July 1930.
74. Tena Holkeboer to My own precious mother, brothers, and sisters, 9 July 1930.
75. Tena Holkeboer to My own precious mother, brothers, and sisters, 9 July 1930.
76. Tena Holkeboer to My own precious mother, brothers, and sisters, 9 July 1930.

operation. As Jean said, 'I believed absolutely that God could take it away as thoroughly as the surgeon's knife.' And *He has done so.*"[77]

After the miraculous disappearance of the mass in her abdomen, Holkeboer continued to experience pain from colitis. The mission doctors prescribed rest, and Holkeboer made plans to go to the popular missionary mountain resort Kuliang, near Fuzhou, for a month in August 1930.[78] Gradually, her health and strength returned, and by the middle of the fall semester of the 1930-31 school year, she could report to her family, "Am thankful to state that my health really seems to be coming back. The old pain does not return any more and I can put in a hard days [sic] work without breaking down afterwards."[79] The semester was ending on a high note, and Holkeboer's good cheer fully returned:

> Have had a most exciting time since I last wrote. Our Middle School Girls went into a Mandarin-speaking oratorical contest with . . . the boys' & girls' high schools of Amoy & Kulangsu . . . Well, the contest took place on Dec. 1 for Senior Middle. There were 26 contestants. One of our girls got 2nd place, another 8th, & the other 9th. But the average of the three was higher than that of any other school, and so as a school we got *first* place! Say, *were* we elated?![80]

About a week later, the school celebrated these achievements in a grand fashion, with a procession through the streets, songs, and firecrackers, among other activities: "*Did* we have a good time!? Say, I wish you could have seen those girls. Stunts, speeches, singing, for three solid hours, & we weren't a bit tired! It's a day long to be remembered by teachers & pupils alike."[81]

Thus, in her second term as an RCA missionary, Holkeboer settled into her role as an educator, faithfully raising up a new generation of Chinese Christian women, and even taking a leadership role beyond the school where she was serving as principal by sitting on the Educational Committee

---

77. Tena Holkeboer to My own precious mother, brothers, and sisters, 9 July 1930.
78. Tena Holkeboer to My own dear family, 5 August 1930.
79. Tena Holkeboer to My own loved ones, 4 November 1930.
80. Tena Holkeboer to My own dear family, 15 December 1930.
81. Tena Holkeboer to My own dear family, 15 December 1930.

of the Chinese Synod.[82] She was now a veteran missionary of fourteen years when she went home for her second furlough in 1934.[83]

The Christian life is often paradoxical—one in which sorrow and danger can coexist with joy and peace. Holkeboer's third term in China, from 1935 to 1941, was such. It was a time of great fruitfulness in her ministry and the work of the Amoy Mission, growing political uncertainty, and, even after many years in the mission field, the pain of separation from family, especially in times of sorrow. Holkeboer began her third term in an atmosphere of spiritual vitality. During the first decades of the twentieth century, the Amoy Mission implemented several new methods of evangelism: Sunday schools for children as well as older church goers, daily kindergartens in churches, vacation Bible schools, and book rooms in some communities. It increased its efforts to publish religious literature by joining with the English Presbyterian Mission and the London Missionary Society to form the South Fukien Religious Tract Society. It held revival meetings, often referred to as "evangelistic campaigns," either led by local RCA missionaries or in collaboration with evangelists of the Young Men's Christian Association (YMCA) from America or independent Chinese preachers such as the renowned Dr. John Song.[84] By the mid-1930s, these efforts were bearing fruit in evident ways.

Holkeber arrived on Gulangyu on September 7, 1935, for the start of her third term and just in time for the opening exercises of the new school year the same day.[85] About a month after her return to the mission field, Holkeboer recounted her activities on a Sunday to her family—meeting with a group of girl students for Christian fellowship at eight in the morning, delivering the message to a congregation of 400 at a church service at 9:30, and teaching a training class for Sunday School teachers after the service, then attending a special service for young people at five in the afternoon and an English service at six.[86] "Oh, there are so many opportunities for service—open doors on every hand!"[87] and variations thereof

---

82. Tena Holkeboer to My own precious family, 30 December 1930.

83. A term of service was seven years, except the first term, which was shortened to five years during Holkeboer's first term with the Amoy Mission; see Holkeboer to Dear, dear loved ones at home, 26 December 1922.

84. De Jong, *The Reformed Church in China*, 188–92.

85. Tena Holkeboer to My own dear family, 13 September 1935.

86. Tena Holkeboer to Dear mother, & sisters, & brothers, 15 October 1935.

87. Tena Holkeboer to Dear mother, & sisters, & brothers, 15 October 1935.

were an often-heard refrain in her letters home from this term. In a letter to one of her sisters in the following spring, she gave further examples of the vibrant spiritual atmosphere permeating the mission and its Chinese churches: a band of women going once or twice a week to visit the prison in Xiamen, a wealthy doctor in Xiamen inviting people to church and visiting and praying with the people whom he invited, a former secretary of the YMCA giving a testimony before officials and influential men of Xiamen on the 25th anniversary of the association's establishment in the city, commitment on the part of Holkeboer and her fellow missionaries in Christian education to focus on the spiritual needs of students by speaking to at least one person each week about spiritual matters, and numerous invitations to preach to large Chinese congregations.[88] Holkeboer was fully immersed in the work of Christian education not only at her school but also in the city's churches, meeting monthly with Christian school leaders and the pastors and elders of Xiamen's churches. All these developments led her to brim with enthusiasm: "Everywhere the churches are filled to overflowing, and many are being brought to Christ. . . . Every Sunday there are literally hundreds going out into Amoy and Kulangsu to bring the gospel message into the homes. . . . Oh dear, . . . you got me started on a subject on which I could write a book!"[89]

Holkeboer's letter home during the school's Easter break in 1936 illustrates her evangelistic zeal, the sense of fulfillment she experienced in the mission field, and the pain of separation from and longing for her family all at the same time. She had received the news of a sister's miscarriage and the death of an uncle prior to her Easter letter:

> "My heart is very heavy tonight, and oh how I *long* for you all! Somehow I just can't *believe* that Chris and Bart have lost their baby . . . It makes my heart *ache* to think that you undergo all these things and I am totally oblivious of your experiences until a month after they have happened . . . The same letter brought the news of uncle E. O.'s homegoing. Once more, I seem to be in a dream—I simply *cannot* realize that both uncle E. O. & aunt Sena are gone. Then I realize the distance which separates us."[90]

Yet, in the same letter, she told of a "happy Easter season" and her taking time during the school break to have individual conversations with students:

88. Tena Holkeboer to Dear Gertrude, 23 March 1936.
89. Tena Holkeboer to Dear Gertrude, 23 March 1936.
90. Tena Holkeboer to Dear, dear home folks, 17 April 1936.

"I am having personal talks with various pupils each morning from 9 to 12 ... Perhaps you wonder why I fill up the mornings this way. Simply because I do not seem to be able to find time for it on regular days. . . . How I *wish* I could introduce you to some of my girls! Some of them would just steal your heart, I am sure."[91] These efforts resulted in great spiritual fruitfulness. Toward the end of the 1936–1937 school year, after a week of regular chapel services and special meetings in the afternoon conducted by an alumna of the school, eighty-two students identified themselves as Christians when invited to stand as a witness, followed by eighty-six students who expressed their desire to accept Christ as their personal Savior when invited to do so.[92] As Holkeboer explained to her family, much faithful prayer and mentoring had preceded this day:

> Much personal work has been done and much prayer, both by individuals and groups, has been offered for a long time. Because of the Bible study and gospel talks at chapel throughout the year we feel that the girls are not taking this step blindly—they understand what they are doing. Whether each one of these 86 is truly converted we cannot say, but their expression certainly means that heart-doors are open and we can work in receptive soil. . . . Surely we can thank and praise God for this assurance of His blessing upon our work.[93]

The fact that a graduate of the school was the speaker of that week's chapel services and special meetings is strong evidence of the abiding spiritual fruit borne by Holkeboer and her Chinese and missionary colleagues in Christian education, one might add.

Holkeboer's leadership responsibilities during her third term of service extended beyond the Amoy Mission itself. The Amoy Mission had collaborated with the English Presbyterian Mission and the London Missionary Society in its work in southern Fujian since the nineteenth century. The most visible form of this ecumenical collaboration was the establishment of the Synod of South Fujian by churches of the Amoy Mission and the English Presbyterian Mission, which held its first regular session in 1894. When the London Missionary Society joined the Synod in 1920, the South Fujian United Church was formed under the direction of the combined synod, now named South Fujian United Synod. In 1927, Chinese churches

---

91. Tena Holkeboer to Dear, dear home folks, 17 April 1936.
92. Tena Holkeboer to Dear mother, Anne, & Grace, 17 June 1937.
93. Tena Holkeboer to Dear mother, Anne, & Grace, 17 June 1937.

of various denominations across the country joined together to form the Church of Christ in China, and the South Fujian United Synod was among the churches that joined and sent delegates.[94] In 1937, Holkeboer and her Chinese colleague Christina Wang were appointed by the Synod to be its delegates to the General Assembly of the Church of Christ in China;[95] the Fourth General Assembly of the Church of Christ in China took place in the port city of Qingdao in Shandong[96] province that year.[97] When war broke out following an armed clash between Chinese and Japanese soldiers near Marco Polo Bridge outside Beiping,[98] Holkeboer had been attending meetings of the General Assembly with Christina Wang. Missionary nurse Nienhuis had made the trip to Qingdao with the two, and the three women had plans to tour Beiping after the conclusion of the meetings. The outbreak of war in north China made them change their plans; they stayed on in Qingdao for a little over a week and made it their vacation before starting on their journey back to Gulangyu.[99]

The outbreak of war between China and Japan changed more than Holkeboer's vacation plans in the summer of 1937. A harbinger of things to come was the harrowing journey back to Xiamen from Qingdao—the trains and train stations crowded with refugees, the separation of Wang from her two Western missionary friends as the latter had to be evacuated from Shanghai, and air raids along the way.[100] Holkeboer's year-end letter home from 1937 had a subdued tone:

> Japan has left us in peace during the Christmas week—fired of [sic] few shells on Sunday, the 26th, but that was all. Without actually firing during that week, I think our Christians forgot their troubles for a few days, and were actually able to enter into the meaning of the Christmas season. There were no grand celebrations and

---

94. De Jong, *The Reformed Church in China*, 100–101, 182–83, 185–86.

95. Holkeboer to Dear mother, Anne, & Grace, 17 June 1937. Holkeboer referred to the South Fujian United Synod as the "Chinese Synod" in her correspondence.

96. Formerly spelled Tsingtao and Shantung, respectively.

97. The Hong Kong Council of the Church of Christ in China, "About Us—Historical Perspective," http://www.hkcccc.org/Eng/1main.php (accessed 2 July 2021).

98. The name of Beijing (formerly spelled Peking) under the GMD, or Nationalist, Government.

99. Tena Holkeboer to Dear Home-folks, 22 July 1937; Tena Holkeboer to Dear home-folks, 6 August 1937.

100. Tena Holkeboer to My own dear family, [August – September 1937]; written on board the S. S. President Hoover.

little exchange of Christmas gifts, but the churches and schools held special services as usual, and much was done for the poor and suffering.[101]

Since no letter from the year 1938 and only one from 1939 survives, there is once again a gap in what can be known. What is known is that the Amoy Mission was actively involved in refugee work on the island of Gulangyu,[102] and that Holkeboer continued to find people's hearts receptive to the gospel. Her New Year letter home from 1940 spoke of a blessed school term— more than fifty students accepted Christ in 1939, and many students were "developing beautiful Christian characters."[103]

The second half of the year 1940 was arguably the most difficult period in Holkeboer's missionary career in China. In addition to the Girls' School, she took on the responsibilities of Tung Wen Institute, filling in for fellow missionary Henry Poppen, who was on furlough, for the 1940–41 school year. Moreover, around the start of the new school term, her sister Anne and her brother Peter became seriously ill. Anne passed away in September 1940, barely a week after she wrote to another sister, asking if she should request to have her furlough a year early, for her next furlough was not due until 1942.[104] Subsequent letters home repeatedly asked her mother and sister Gertrude whether she should request early furlough.[105] Her sorrow and conflicting thoughts were poignantly expressed in these lines:

> Oh, mother, mother, how *hard* it is to be separated from you all. If it were not for God's special grace I simply could not bear it! Thank God, He spared Peter to us for the present. But oh, *how* I want to go home at once! And yet—is it right? Is it running away from duty? I pray that God may make His way clear, so that I may not mistake His will. With two big schools on my hands during these critical times it does not seem right to leave at once. Our workers

---

101. Tena Holkeboer to Dear mother & sisters, 30 December 1937.

102. Please see the chapter "Faith and Humanitarian Aid in Wartime China, 1937–1941" by Claire Barrett in this volume.

103. Tena Holkeboer to Dear Home-folks, 2 January 1940.

104. Tena Holkeboer to Dearest sister, 7 September [1940]; Tena Holkeboer to Dearest, dearest mother, 18 September [1940].

105. Tena Holkeboer to Dearest sister [Gertrude], 18 Septermber [1940]; Tena Holkeboer to Precious, precious mother, 25 September [1940]; Tena Holkeboer to Mother dear, 2 October [1940].

are already so very few and all are carrying loads almost too heavy for them.[106]

After she finally decided to request early furlough, she learned that the U.S. government was now advising evacuation in response to the prospect of war with Japan, which caused another dilemma for Holkeboer; for now there was the possibility that she may not be allowed to return to China should war break out between the U.S. and Japan.[107] The issue was resolved, however, when the Board moved up the furloughs of all missionaries who were due to take them in 1942 by one year. Yet, in a cruel twist of events, Peter died before the news that Holkeboer would be home in 1941 could reach her family in Michigan.[108] The news of Peter's death came as a severe blow. Both pain and quiet resignation to God's mysterious ways were revealed in a letter to her mother and sister Gertrude written a few days after the arrival of the news:

> It is the hardest trial I have ever met. The sense of God's presence did not leave me, but His hand was laid on me in chastisement so heavy that it seemed more than I could bear. All night it poured, thunder, & there was severe lightning, which but seemed to typify God's wrath. I could glean no comfort from God's Word. The only words that milled round in my mind all night long were those of Naomi, "Call me not Naomi, but Marah, for the Lord hath dealt bitterly with me." They gave me a dose of sleeping medicine & 10 gr. of aspirin, but to no avail. The next day I ached from head to foot so that it was impossible to be up. . . .
>
> And oh, mother mine, what can I say to comfort you? God has asked of you two of your children in such a short period of time. It is hard to understand why he should ask this, but when we cannot see, we must simply trust. "God's way *is* the best way," even though it is a hard way. And it is sweet to think that now Anne & Peter are reunited with papa on the other shore, isn't it? As our family circle decreases here, it increases on the other side![109]

The Pacific War made Holkeboer's third furlough a long one. She left Gulangyu in 1941 and had to wait till 1943 to be given permission to travel back to Asia by a long and circuitous sea route that would first take her to Lisbon, Portugal, then Portuguese East Africa and Durban, South Africa,

106. Tena Holkeboer to Mother dearest, 10 October 1940.
107. Tena Holkeober to Precious mother and Gertrude, 16 October [1940].
108. Tena Holkeboer to Dearest mother, brothers, and sisters, 24 January 1941.
109. Tena Holkeboer to Precious mother & Gertrude, 27 January 1941.

and finally land her in Calcutta,[110] India. She wanted to go on to China from there, but wartime conditions made it impossible, and she served in the RCA's Arcot Mission in India until she was given permission to fly to Shanghai on a military plane in December 1945.[111] Holkeboer arrived on Gulangyu on January 9, 1946, after a harrowing journey from Shanghai that included near shipwrecks, attacks by pirates, rats in bed, hunger, and cold.[112] The Girls' School on Gulangyu had continued to operate under Chinese leadership during the missionaries' absence, even though many other RCA institutions had stopped functioning under Japanese occupation.

Holkeboer joined the Tong'an station sometime in the second half of 1946, and remarkably, now in her fifties, she embarked on a new initiative to strengthen rural churches and evangelize the countryside. She did this work with Christina Wang and another Chinese colleague, Miss Ho, and it involved much traveling and physical hardship, as described in a letter home in the early stages of the work:

> We'll spend 2 weeks in Lengna[113] holding meetings & then go on to Chiang-peng[114] where we hope to have another month's experiment in village work. That means I won't get back to Amoy & Tungan, D.V., till the end of April. Two months on the road, with rice three times a day & many physical discomforts too numerous to mention—this will be a new experience for me. You will be glad to know I have an air mattress to take with me. That will ease my weary old bones a bit—boards are *so hard*!!![115]

This was hardship willingly taken on and of her own initiative. It was, in a sense, work that she would have liked to do when she was a young missionary. Her typical Holkeboer spirit shone through in her explanation to her concerned mother:

> As for the work I am doing—no one is forcing me. I just feel called to do what I can to meet a crying need. . . . I wish I could have started this when I was younger, but at that time the school was

110. Modern-day Kolkata.

111. Kwantes, *She Has Done a Beautiful Thing for Me*, 189–191.

112. Kwantes, 191; Tena Holkeboer to Dear Friends, 29 December 1945; Tena Holkeboer to Dear Friends, 21 January 1946.

113. Modern-day Longyan.

114. Modern-day Zhangping.

115. Tena Holkeboer to Precious mother & Gertrude, 3 March 1947. Chinese beds traditionally consisted of wooden boards, even for the well-to-do.

unable to do without me. When Miss Chen returns from (furlough) study in America, I hope I can give the rest of my days to preaching the gospel & helping prepare others to do so. The doors are wide open, but the workers are so desperately few.[116]

Holkeboer had China in mind when she penned the words "the rest of my days," but it was not meant to be, for in a year's time she would have to take an early furlough for health reasons:

> Am not sick, but the nervous tension of the past five years has been a little more than I could take, and it seems time to call a halt. Dr. Holleman. . .strongly advises me to leave as soon as Carol Chen gets back. . . . It will be exactly 5 years in Oct. that I left home. I'm supposed to do 5 years and eight months, so the term is somewhat shortened. But I am so troubled with insomnia & nervous headaches that it seems wise to stop in time rather than break down.[117]

Thus, Holkeboer left China in 1948, for what she expected to be another furlough. It was in fact the closure of her missionary career in China,[118] for Communist forces would prevail in 1949, ending the Chinese Civil War, which had been fought intermittently since 1927, and the last missionaries of the Amoy Mission would leave China in 1951.

In the course of Holkeboer's twenty-eight-year missionary career in China, one sees the development of a single female missionary from an inexperienced young woman to an accomplished leader. Holkeboer's state as a single woman allowed her to develop her abilities and take on leadership roles to a far greater extent than was possible for married women missionaries in her era—serving as a school principal, sitting on various mission committees, and representing the South Fujian United Synod at the General Assembly of the Church of Christ in China, among her numerous positions of responsibility. Her faith, piety, singleness of purpose, sense of calling, and strength of will shone forth through times of illness, physical hardship, sorrow, and loneliness. Single women missionaries were an important pillar in the Protestant missionary movement. In the years 1918, 1928, 1938, and 1941, unmarried women missionaries outnumbered married women missionaries by 46:42, 58:57, 49:42, and 47:40, respectively, in

---

116. Tena Holkeboer to Dear mother & Gertrude, 17 May 1947.

117. Tena Holkeboer to Dear mother & Gertrude, Grace & Hero, 15 April 1948.

118. Holkeboer's missionary career did not conclude with the end of the missionary era in China, however; she continued to minister among Chinese in the Philippines for another decade.

all the foreign mission fields of the RCA combined.[119] They constituted a "religious order" that has not been recognized as such. Holkeboer's experiences in China offer a glimpse into the internal world of these remarkable women and bring to the foreground their contributions to the cause of the gospel.

Bibliography

Primary Sources

Board of Foreign Missions, Reformed Church in America. *One Hundred and Tenth Annual Report*. New York: Reformed Church Headquarters, 1942.

Tena Holkeboer Papers. W88-0055. Joint Archives of Holland, Holland, MI.

Secondary Sources

De Jong, Gerald Francis. *The Reformed Church in China, 1842–1951*. Historical Series of the Reformed Church in America 22. Grand Rapids: Eerdmans, 1992.

Kwantes, Anne C. *She Has Done a Beautiful Thing for Me: Portraits of Christian Women in Asia*. Manila, Philippines: OMF Literature, 2005.

Latourette, Kenneth Scott. *A History of Christian Missions in China*. New York: Macmillan, 1929.

---

119. Board of Foreign Missions, Reformed Church in America, *One Hundred and Tenth Annual Report*, 15. It was the 1942 joint report of the denomination's Board of Foreign Missions and Woman's Board of Foreign Missions to the General Synod.

6

Faith and Humanitarian Aid in Wartime China, 1937–1941

Claire Barrett

A 1940 ARTICLE IN *The Intelligencer-Leader*, a weekly magazine of the Reformed Church in America (RCA), states with a sense of gravity, "The heroism of these Christian missionaries in China, carrying on their mission of relief and service to millions of suffering Chinese, will remain one of the great chapters of the history of the Christian Church."[1] The Second Sino-Japanese War (1937–1945) and World War II (1939–1945) led to an estimated ten to twenty million Chinese civilian deaths. The humanitarian aid provided by RCA missionaries in China was a stark contrast to the brutality seen not only in combat, but also in atrocities committed by the Japanese army against Chinese civilians. The missionaries' work during this time was not limited to the preaching of the Gospel. It demonstrated tangibly the Word of God by meeting practical needs. From an early date, RCA missionaries in China had been involved in education and medical work, which was justified by Scripture's emphasis on the obligation of Christians to do good.[2] However, the aid and assistance given during the Second Sino-Japanese War far exceeded any previous effort. As this chapter shows,

1. "For China. . ." *The Intelligencer-Leader*, 19 January 1940.
2. De Jong, *The Reformed Church in China*, xii.

the relief provided by RCA missionaries met a desperate need that the Chinese government was unable to address. A reexamination of the RCA's refugee work on the island of Gulangyu[3] from the start of the Second Sino-Japanese War to the missionaries' internment in 1941 would eventually contribute to altering modern ideas of Western missionaries in China.

The RCA began its missionary work in China in 1842 on the island of Xiamen.[4] Established by the Reverend David Abeel, the Amoy Mission was located on the southeast coast of China and headquartered on the small island of Gulangyu. It became the foundation for large-scale missionary efforts as Abeel and the missionaries who followed him labored to spread the Christian message and win souls for Christ.[5] This mission also developed educational and medical institutions, which would play a vital role in refugee work during the Second Sino-Japanese War.

The island of Gulangyu is located a few miles off mainland China in Fujian province, about 300 miles north of Hong Kong, and 550 miles south of Shanghai. Gulangyu lies southwest of the larger island of Xiamen. By providing an ideal location for the transportation of goods and people by ferries, it served the missionaries and, after 1937, refugees, well. The area of the small island is only 0.73 square mile. Its pre-war population numbered only several thousand, which in 1938 rose by more than ten times due to a sudden influx of refugees.

The creation of international settlements began with the signing of the Treaty of Nanjing on August 29, 1842, at the end of the First Opium War between Britain and China from 1839 to 1842. Gulangyu was officially designated one such settlement in 1903, subsequently becoming a Western oasis as international religious groups, commercial shipping firms, financial institutions, consulates—including one representing the United States—were established on the island. Thus, in the early twentieth century an international community emerged on the island, which was not under the direct control of the Chinese, but run by the nationals of several countries, including Britain, America, and Japan. Within a year after the start of hostilities between Japan and China in 1937, the entire region of eastern China came under Japanese control, including the city of Xiamen. Tens

---

3. Gulangyu, a small island off the coast of the island of Xiamen, was known to RCA missionaries of the time as Kulangsu.

4. Known to RCA missionaries of the time as Amoy; hence, the RCA's mission there was called the Amoy Mission. Xiamen, or Amoy, the city, encompasses both the island of Xiamen and the island of Gulangyu.

5. De Jong, *The Reformed Church in China*, xii.

of thousands of Chinese who fled from Xiamen went to Gulangyu, which, until the end of 1941, offered a measure of security from Japanese forces because of its international status.[6]

Among the residents of the international settlement on Gulangyu were Japanese citizens. In 1938, Japanese nationals on the island called upon the Japanese government for more troops to protect them. Missionary nurse Alma Vander Meer[7] recalled in an interview many years later, "the foreign population got together with the municipal council and voted that [they] too should call upon other governments to send troops. So... France and England and the United States each had the same amount as the Japanese troops."[8] Although conditions would soon deteriorate and brutality by the Japanese army abounded, the distinction of being an international settlement with a significant foreign population allowed Gulangyu to provide a safer existence for the Chinese who took refuge on the island and thereby escaped the fate of those in cities like Nanjing during the war.[9]

The Chinese Government

The outbreak of the Second Sino-Japanese War was not the first instance of Japan's territorial aggression on the Chinese mainland, for in 1931, Japan had invaded Manchuria. The 1937 conflict ended any chance for Chiang Kai-shek, leader of the Chinese Nationalist Party,[10] to create a strong, cen-

---

6. Spence, *The Search for Modern China*, 419–25; De Jong, *The Reformed Church in China*, 255–6; White, ed., *Protestantism in Xiamen*, 51–8.

7. Alma Vander Meer (née Mathiesen) was born in Skandenburg, Denmark, on 22 April 1894, and commissioned as a medical missionary to China in September 1923. In 1929, during her furlough, she married American missionary William Vander Meer. She returned to the United States in 1942, during the war, but went back to China in 1946. In March 1951, she left China after petitioning the new Communist regime for permission to leave.

8. Alma Vander Meer, interview by David M. Vander Haar, transcript, 28, The Old China Hands Oral History Project (1976–1977), H88–0113, Joint Archives of Holland, Holland, MI.

9. The Japanese entered the city of Nanjing (formerly known as Nanking) on 13 December 1937. The widespread destruction, murder, and rape in the seven weeks that followed rank among the worst in the history of modern warfare. Suping Lu cites the findings of the International Military Tribunal for the Far East (1948) on the "Rape of Nanjing"—over 200,000 murders of civilians and prisoners of war and approximately 20,000 cases of rape against women and girls—in *A Mission under Duress*, ix.

10. Also known as the Kuomintang, or Guomindang. I will be using this English

tralized nation-state. In the face of rising nationalistic and anti-Japanese sentiment, Chiang Kai-shek's political agenda to unify China first—that is, to destroy the Communist movement—and fight Japanese invasion second failed, and he entered an uneasy and brief alliance with the Communists out of necessity. China faced a multitude of problems at the onset of the conflict. The nation was broken up into areas under Nationalist, Communist, and warlord control. In *China at War: Regions of China, 1937–1945*, Diana Lary argues, "The de facto division of China into so many different regions underlines the fact that there was no functioning nationwide system of government during the war, but instead a series of discrete regimes whose shape and size often changed."[11]

Without assistance from their national leaders, Chinese refugees fleeing from the Japanese onslaught found a unique ally in Christian missionaries. Prior to 1941, before the United States declared war on Japan, American citizens had been neutral foreign nationals in China. This important distinction provided RCA missionaries a measure of safety in the face of an invading army. The missionaries' evangelistic, educational, and medical work prior to the outbreak of hostilities allowed them to quickly establish a relief network once the need arose.

The Japanese Invasion

On May 10, 1938, the Japanese invaded Xiamen. In his diary, Dr. Clarence Holleman wrote about the events of that day:

> 4 A.M. the bombardment really began in earnest . . . it is reported that some 200 Japanese soldiers have landed under cover of darkness. From that time on throughout the day we are deafened by the roar of planes, diving and zooming, dropping bombs and firing machine guns, the anti-aircraft from below and a million other sounds that are a mixture of them all.[12]

By the next day, May 11, the Japanese had easily taken Xiamen and, in doing so, created a humanitarian crisis. The war had cut off communication

---

translation rather than the transliterated Chinese term.

11. MacKinnon, Lary, and Vogel, eds., *China at War*, 12.

12. Clarence H. Holleman, "Extracts from a Diary, May 10," *The Intelligencer-Leader*, 1 July 1938. Dr. Holleman (1890–1973) was a medical missionary of the Amoy Mission from 1919 to 1941 and from 1946 to late 1949 or early 1950; see De Jong, *The Reformed Church in China*, 320-22.

between Xiamen and the rest of the world. By Japanese order, the telephone lines and telegraph offices were destroyed. Many Chinese fled from Xiamen or were shot in their attempt to escape. Gulangyu was the first destination of those who fled, generating a huge demand for the dwindling food and water resources on the small island. Despite the chaos that erupted in that foreign land, the Amoy Mission remained. Dr. Holleman wrote that even in those circumstances, "we foreigners are not afraid for ourselves, but for those under our care."[13] The focus was not on the missionaries themselves, but on the imminent humanitarian crisis.

In the initial days following the invasion, foreigners on the island, missionaries among them, organized an International Relief Committee, which replaced a Chinese committee that had failed to operate. The new committee was composed of four Westerners and five Chinese, with the Reverend Henry Poppen as chairman.[14] Working together with the Japanese military, Chinese remaining on Gulangyu and in Xiamen, Chinese expatriates in Southeast Asia, and the American and British governments, the members of the Amoy Mission would provide extensive aid in the form of medical care, food, shelter, schooling, and spiritual instruction.

Missionary doctor Clarence Holleman stated that while only five percent or less of the population on the island of Gulangyu were Christian, "more than 90 percent of the leadership and relief work was conducted by them."[15] However, even though the leadership was provided by missionaries, it was Chinese who cooked the meals and cleaned for the refugees; they also translated for many of the missionaries, an essential function in the refugee camps that were quickly set up.[16] Alma Vander Meer would recall in her retirement that "on the island of Kulangsu tents were erected and the Chinese organized themselves into working squads, some for cleaning, and some for cooking, et cetera."[17] The Committee promptly directed that every building on Gulangyu be put to use to house refugees. On the small

13. Holleman, "Extracts from a Diary, May 12," *The Intelligencer-Leader*, 1 July 1938.

14. Poppen was an RCA missionary to China from 1918 to 1951; "Quotations from diary of Dr. C. H. Holleman, Kulangsu, Amoy, China, May 13, 1938," typescript, 3–4, folder "Writings," Clarence H. Holleman Papers, W95-1196, Joint Archives of Holland.

15. "Quotations from diary of Dr. C. H. Holleman, Kulangsu, Amoy, China, May 13, 1938," typescript, 3.

16. David Angus, interview by Marc Baer, Claire Barrett, Katelyn Dickerson, Victoria Longfield, and Gloria Tseng, 21 July 2014, Hope College, Holland, MI. Angus was born in Xiamen in 1933 and spent the first eight years of his life there.

17. Alma Vander Meer, interview, transcript, 28.

island, refugees occupied every church, school, factory, temple, and vacant residence. According to Poppen, chairman of the Committee, "During the first two nights thousands slept out in the open, in doorways, sheltered spots along the streets and alleys, in most any place where they lay their heads."[18] In the next few months, mat sheds would be erected for those without shelter.

Medical Needs

From the outset of its missionary work in Xiamen, meeting medical needs was an important objective for the RCA. The RCA's Amoy Mission operated two adjacent hospitals on Gulangyu: Hope and Wilhelmina. During wartime the fees for services were either kept very low or waived altogether. The missionary hospitals on Gulangyu were inundated with wounded Chinese civilians and soldiers. By nightfall on May 10, the small Wilhelmina hospital had received 130 patients. The staff, overwhelmed by the overflow of patients, recruited students from the mission's middle school for girls, who, according to Dr. Holleman, "completed a first aid course at our hospital just a few weeks ago, are helping bravely."[19] Roughly one month after the Japanese occupation of Xiamen, *The Intelligencer-Leader* published observations of RCA missionaries in China commenting on the rising number of refugees flocking to Gulangyu, where the "wounded and the dying, all were brought in, doubling the normal capacity of our hospital."[20] Although the small island's facilities were stretched thin, the missionaries, doctors and nurses among them, worked unremittingly for the next four years.

In a letter published in *The Intelligencer-Leader*, Poppen approximated that after the Japanese forces captured Xiamen, the island of Gulangyu saw an influx of approximately 60,000 refugees from the city. With its hot climate and now over-population, the fear of an outbreak of diseases such as cholera and typhoid in the camps was a foremost concern to the doctors and nurses on the island. Urgent calls for assistance were sent out, and by June 6, 1938, the missionaries had received from the Lord Mayor's Fund of London a supply of cholera and typhoid vaccine, enough for 50,000 injections. Poppen estimated that the medical staff had already given more

18. Henry A. Poppen, "Inasmuch...," *The Intelligencer-Leader*, 7 July 1939.
19. Holleman, "Extracts from a Diary, May 10."
20. Henry A. Poppen, "Dear Friends in the Homeland," *Intelligencer-Leader*, 29 July 1938.

than 15,000 injections at the time of writing.[21] Throughout the Japanese occupation, only the mission's hospitals could obtain medical supplies. Even so, getting them through the Japanese checkpoints was very difficult. In a speech to the Shanghai Tiffin Club in New York in the summer of 1942, Robert W. Barnett, who had traveled to China on behalf of United China Relief[22] earlier that year, remarked that "a basic case underlying most of the problems which I observed was the breakdown of transportation."[23] Cut off from mainland China and occupied by a hostile nation, it was essential for those carrying out relief work on Gulangyu to work not only with the Japanese, but also with the Chinese, the British, and the Americans.

Multi-government Cooperation and Aid

The neutrality of the missionaries was crucial to maintaining relationships with both Chinese and Japanese governments, making possible their actions done out of moral and religious conviction and saving the lives of many Chinese refugees. After the agonizing twenty-four hours of bombardment inflicted by the Japanese invasion on May 10, 1938, few residents on Gulangyu had food, and even fewer had access to water, for the Japanese had cut off the water supply. However, the U.S. Navy and the American Consul came to the aid of both the missionaries and the refugees. A month after the invasion, Poppen wrote to supporters in America, "Captain Quynn of the U.S.S. Ashville hoisted the stars and stripes over the water boat and went to Amoy for water. Since then the Japanese Admiral has given permission to supply Kulangsu with water and water is now being supplied by the Japanese Navy."[24] Furthermore, working with the Red Cross, the missionaries negotiated with the Japanese to allow them to take a boat from Gulangyu to the mainland, so that those living in the remote rural areas could receive the necessary supplies. Thus, the missionaries on the islands of Gulangyu and Xiamen played an essential role by acting as an intermediary with the

21. Henry A. Poppen, "From a letter from Mr. H. A. Poppen, June 6th, sent by China Clipper," *The Intelligencer-Leader*, 1 July 1938; Poppen, "Inasmuch. . . ."

22. Founded in 1941 in New York City for the purpose of raising funds to help the Chinese people in times of national crisis; participating organizations included the American Bureau for Medical Aid to China, the Associated Boards for Christian Colleges in China, the China Emergency Relief Committee, the Church Committee for China Relief, and the China Aid Council.

23. Barnett, "Isolated China," 167–69.

24. Poppen, "Dear Friends in the Homeland."

Japanese to obtain goods and medical supplies not only for the islands, but also for those on the mainland.

The missionaries were able to provide relief in the form of medicine, clothing, food, and water by working in conjunction with churches in the United States, Japanese occupation authorities, the Chinese government, Chinese associated with the mission on the islands of Xiamen and Gulangyu and up-country, overseas Chinese, Americans, and British. Establishing lines of communication in the early days of the occupation was essential to facilitating humanitarian aid. The Church Committee for China Relief[25] made an urgent appeal in North America, and the RCA participated actively in this multi-denominational relief effort for China. The RCA's 1938 Annual Report of the Board of Foreign Missions noted that "it became apparent early last fall that there would be serious need of civilian relief in China and . . . an appeal for $15,000 was sent out to the Churches."[26] Three hundred and sixteen churches responded to the request and by May 11, 1938, $15,961.55 had been received. Of this amount, $6,550 was sent to the National Christian Council of China for refugee camps and other relief needs.[27] Amoy missionaries in China and their supporters in America were doing their part in stemming the staggering humanitarian crisis that was occurring in war-torn China.

Amoy missionaries stationed up-country and those stationed on Gulangyu reinforced each other's efforts. In Zhangzhou,[28] the missionaries created a British-American relief committee that facilitated the supply of fuel and vegetables to Gulangyu.[29] There, they arranged for relief boats to carry supplies to the refugees on Gulangyu. By the end of September 1938, $20,000[30] worth of supplies had been sent there, and it was estimated that future shipments would require around $3,000 per month.[31] The Japa-

---

25. The Church Committee for China Relief (1938–44) was constituted by the Federal Council of the Churches of Christ in America, the Foreign Missions Conference of North America, and the China Famine Relief.

26. Board of Foreign Missions, Reformed Church in America, *One Hundred and Sixth Annual Report*, 6.

27. Board of Foreign Missions, Reformed Church in America, *One Hundred and Sixth Annual Report*, 6.

28. Formerly known variously as Changchow or Chiang-chiu to RCA missionaries.

29. "News from the Front," *The Intelligencer-Leader*, 17 February 1939.

30. The Mexican silver dollar is referred to specifically in this source, but not others.

31. William Angus, "Latest News from Amoy," *The Intelligencer-Leader*, 6 January 1939.

nese occupation authorities responded to the initial pleas for assistance addressed to the Japanese Consul General by supplying the mission with vaccines for contagious diseases. Poppen wrote in *The Intelligencer-Leader* that within a month of the invasion, the Japanese Navy "donated 304 bags of rice, 100 bags of flour, 98 bags of sugar, 40 bags of salt and 20 cases of soy towards relief of refugees on Kulangsu."[32] The International Relief Committee on the island sent radio messages through British and American warships requesting help, with the result that "General Chiang Kai-Shek responded with $100,000; Overseas Chinese in Singapore and the Straits and Manila sent funds and shipped rice; to date more than $300,000 has been received in addition to large quantities of rice; 41,000 are being supplied with two meals per day; a milk depot supplies milk to babies; an emergency hospital and two clinics have been opened."[33]

Thus, the work of the missionaries through the International Relief Committee were critical during this period. Overseas Chinese donated rice, money, and clothing, sending them through one of the few channels available—the missionaries. As mentioned above, the Nationalist government had donated $100,000 to the relief effort organized by the missionaries.[34] While the Chinese government donated money, it was the missionaries on the ground who budgeted and cared for the needs of the refugees. Appeals to Chinese living in Singapore and Manila yielded not only money and food, but also clothes for the refugees. Poppen reported that during the winter of 1938–39, "$15,000 worth of wool, cloth and thread was purchased in Shanghai and a group of more than twenty women from the camps were set to work to make these quilts."[35] Donations flooded in, and it was "a common sight to see refugee ladies dressed in fur collared coats and swank London frocks parading the streets."[36] In 1939, there were approximately 800 children who acquired three new garments of clothing each as the seasons changed, which meant sorting more than 2,000 articles of clothing to distribute within the camps.[37]

---

32. Poppen, "From a letter."
33. Poppen, "Dear Friends in the Homeland."
34. Poppen, "From a letter."
35. Poppen, "Inasmuch..."
36. Poppen, "Inasmuch..."
37. Edna K. Beckman, "Clothing Needy Chinese Children," *The Intelligencer-Leader*, 9 June 1939.

The missionaries not only provided aid in the form of clothing; they also employed creative methods to provide safety for the refugees. Throughout the course of the conflict, the missionaries used existing British and American flags or sewed new ones. Recognizing that the Japanese would be more hesitant to bomb an area they believed was under American or British aegis, the missionaries used the flags to protect themselves and the refugees. At the Amoy Mission's Zhangzhou station, missionaries were quick to realize the reluctance of the Chinese in the city to seek help at the mission hospital for fear of being bombed; therefore, it relocated the hospital to the mission's seminary buildings, which were adjacent to the property of the London Missionary Society, where the British flag was flown. William Angus noted, "Confidence in the British flag has brought them to the hospital at its new location until facilities have been taxed to the limit."[38] It was commonplace to use the flags of these Western powers to provide a modicum of safety for both missionaries and Chinese. William Vander Meer described the situation in Zhangzhou: "During the attack on Amoy, the interior cities were bombed several times daily.... Huge American flags had to be prepared and so placed as to be visible from both the air and the ground."[39] Even so, RCA mission property in Zhangzhou still suffered damage by Japanese bombs in the second half of 1939.[40] Albeit not a perfect guarantee, British and American flags were among the ingenious methods used by missionaries to protect themselves and the Chinese in their care.

Food Supply

Initially in 1938, 90,000 meals a day were provided to the refugees on Gulangyu in the form of rice and beans mixed with soy sauce, with recipients providing their own utensils and bowls.[41] This was made possible by two canning factories on the island being made available for the preparation of food, with the staff of each factory and volunteers from the refugee camps providing the necessary labor, and kerosene tins supplied by the Standard Vacuum Oil Company and the Asiatic Oil Company being used for the

38. Angus, "Latest News from Amoy."

39. "News from the Front."

40. Henry A. Poppen, "Bombs and Hospitals," *The Intelligencer-Leader*, 20 October 1939.

41. Poppen, "Inasmuch..."

distribution of food.[42] One important concern was to provide nourishment for underfed mothers and their infants. A milk clinic was opened soon after the camps had been set up, and the milk and food distributed by the clinic were supplied partially by the Chinese Red Cross Society, the International Red Cross, and the Lord Mayor's Fund of London. By January 6, 1939, missionary nurse Jessie M. Platz would be caring for 150 undernourished babies and their mothers.[43] Milk, bean milk, and tonics were used for as long as the camps remained open to alleviate the undernourishment of the newborn population.

The Japanese naval blockade on China, which began with the outbreak of the Second Sino-Japanese War in 1937, caused hardship for missionaries and refugees. Communication with mainland China had been essentially cut off. The food supply from the island of Xiamen to Gulangyu was meager, since Xiamen itself was running out of food. Worse still were the prices of commodities. Costs of all foodstuffs had doubled and, in some cases, tripled. Two years into the war, Poppen noted that the sudden depreciation of the Chinese dollar made importing from Hongkong and Singapore prohibitive, and that fuel for cooking was almost exhausted.[44] Yet, the situation would have been worse if not for the five thousand bags of rice that had been brought with the help of the British and American navies from warehouses in the ports of Xiamen to Gulangyu in the aftermath of the Japanese capture of Xiamen, following appeals sent by radiogram to overseas Chinese in Singapore and Manila.[45]

Housing

When the Japanese occupation of Xiamen began in 1938, missionaries of the Amoy Mission cleared every available building on Gulangyu to accommodate the influx of refugees. In addition, huts, tents, and mat sheds were erected to house these displaced Chinese. Alongside the missionaries, Chinese helpers organized themselves into cleaning and cooking divisions to assist in the running of the camps. Clarence Holleman noted that there were fifty-two camps, each ranging from 500 to 3,000 people.[46] At

42. Poppen, "Inasmuch..."
43. Angus, "Latest News from Amoy."
44. Henry A. Poppen, "Amoy Notes," *The Intelligencer-Leader*, August 11, 1939.
45. Poppen, "Inasmuch..."
46. "Quotations from diary of Dr. C. H. Holleman, Kulangsu, Amoy, China,"

the height of the refugee crisis in 1938, Gulangyu "housed" approximately 60,000 refugees. However, that number fluctuated monthly. In a letter to supporters quoted in the denomination's magazine, Vander Meer approximated that in early 1939 there were about 14,000 refugees left and the number of camps on the island had been reduced to twelve. By the middle of the year, Poppen was able to report that only 7,500 refugees remained in the camps, representing a nearly fifty percent decrease. The reduction was largely attributable to refugees leaving the camps for the mainland. Even so, finding enough shelter for the large number of Chinese fleeing the Japanese remained an issue throughout the war. Thousands of Chinese, aided by the missionaries, left Xiamen and Gulangyu for relatively safer locations in Southeast Asia, such as Singapore and Manila. However, as soon as they left, their places in the camps were immediately filled by others.[47]

This massive migration led Poppen to observe, "Never in human history has the number of refugees been as large as it is today in the Year of Our Lord 1939. In China it is estimated that between 50,000,000 to 60,000,000 people have been forced from their homes by war, man's inhumanity to man, and are now either in refugee camps or wandering about in want of shelter, food, medical aid, and love."[48] However, such large numbers in the camps offered innumerable opportunities to provide schooling to many children who had never attended school, as well as a chance to share the Gospel.

Education and Evangelization

While the physical needs of the refugees on Gulangyu received primary attention, their spiritual and educational needs were also attended to. By October 11, 1938, 800 refugee children were enrolled in the seven different schools on Gulangyu and were being taught the three "Rs" of reading, writing, and arithmetic.[49] By July 7, 1939, more than 2,000 children were enrolled in schools set up for the refugees, conducted in large part by volunteer teachers as well as former students of the mission schools.[50] The war had exposed the Chinese to the Gospel, and in their distress it had opened

---

typescript, 4.
    47. "News from the Front"; Poppen, "Inasmuch . . ."
    48. Poppen, "Inasmuch . . ."
    49. Angus, "Latest News from Amoy."
    50. Poppen, "Inasmuch . . ."

their hearts and minds to the message of God. Even in the uncertain circumstances created by the war, the Amoy Mission's educational work continued apace. Angus reported robust enrollment at the schools run by the mission on Gulangyu and up-country. At the up-country station of Tong'an, "Dr. Frank Eckerson and the Chinese Christian leaders...have been engaged in Christian work among the refugees and report wonderful opportunities to preach the Gospel..."[51] Just as they appealed to overseas Chinese to contribute money, food, and clothing to keep the refugee camps running, the missionaries also made special appeals to Chinese living abroad to fund the schools. In 1939, a Chinese businessman in Singapore gave a gift of $20,000 for the education of the children in the refugee camps.[52] There were many children among the refugees, and the missionaries felt that it was necessary to give the children an opportunity for some schooling.

Historical Witness

An essential role that missionaries in Xiamen and elsewhere throughout China played was that of a historical witness and a voice against Japanese wartime savagery. Their records were instrumental at the post-war Tokyo War Crimes Trials, more formally known as the International Military Tribunal for the Far East (1946–48), as well as subsequent Chinese trials of Japanese war criminals. Miner Searle Bates, then the Chairman of the Emergency Committee of the University of Nanking, wrote directly to the Japanese Embassy cataloguing Japanese abuses against those seeking safety at the university. In a letter written to the Japanese Embassy a few days after Japanese troops had entered the city of Nanjing, Dr. Bates said indignantly, "the reign of terror and brutality continues in the plain view of your buildings and among your own neighbors . . . at the library building . . . soldiers raped several women," and implored the Japanese government to rein back the conduct of its soldiers and "give the conquered people a chance to live and work under good order."[53] In his letter to the American consul in January 1938, which was forwarded to Washington, Bates wrote

---

51. Angus, "Latest News from Amoy."
52. Poppen, "Inasmuch . . ."
53. Miner Searle Bates to Officers of the Japanese Embassy, Nanking, 17 December 1937, RG 10: Box 4 Folder 59: "Japanese Embassy, Nanking 1937–1939, Japanese Embassy, Shanghai 1938," The Nanking Massacre Archival Project, Yale Divinity School Library, last modified 29 May 2020, https://web.library.yale.edu/divinity/nanking/documents/.

that the University of Nanking was sheltering 30,000 refugees and that this aid had been "tenaciously maintained amid dishonor by soldiers, murdering, wounding, wholesale raping, resulting in violent terror."[54] Bates fearlessly chronicled Japanese atrocities, advocating for Chinese victims to the best of his ability in a perilous situation. Likewise, the missionaries of the Amoy Mission were the last resort of the refugees on Gulangyu in the face of an uncertain fate.

Information about the war in China reached the American public and the U.S. government by way of letters written by missionaries. A forty-five-page document prepared by Wynn C. Fairfield of the American Board of Commissioners for Foreign Missions[55] provided the Department of State with excerpts of letters from missionaries, documenting their war experiences.[56] Shortly after what is now remembered as the Rape of Nanjing, the Foreign Missions Conference of North America[57] felt duty-bound to publish the scores of letters from missionaries who were in Nanjing during the war. This led to their publication in *Reader's Digest*, where passages from a missionary surgeon who described the Japanese occupation as "this modern 'Dante's Inferno,' written in huge letters with blood and rape,"[58] caught the public's attention. Although these letters home and to the U.S. government did not alter the course of the war as the missionaries had hoped, they served as a testament to the atrocities committed by the Japanese army--still unforgotten today, even with the passage of time.

Religious Conviction and the Missionaries

To be a follower of Christ requires both action and faith, even in the face of extraordinary hardship. The RCA missionaries were persistently motivated to help those in great need, thus personifying God's message. Throughout the course of the Second Sino-Japanese War and World War II, the missionaries reflected Christ and believed that if they wavered in their duty to

---

54. Quoted in Varg, *Missionaries, Chinese, and Diplomats*, 260-1.

55. Formed by Congregationalists in Massachusetts in 1810, the American Board of Commissioners for Foreign Missions was America's first foreign mission society and the predecessor of the United Church Board for World Ministries (1957-).

56. Varg, *Missionaries, Chinese, and Diplomats*, 261.

57. The Foreign Missions Conference of North America (1893-1952) was an association made up of participating foreign mission boards from the United States and Canada.

58. Quoted in Varg, *Missionaries, Chinese, and Diplomats*, 260.

the refugees, it would be a break with their beliefs as Christians. Moreover, they were motivated not only by a faith commitment but also by their own humanity.

Following the outbreak of the Sino-Japanese conflict in 1937, all but a handful of RCA missionaries refused to heed the U.S. government's calls to leave China, believing that it was their Christian duty to remain. The 1938 Annual Report of the RCA Board of Foreign Missions states, "in the whole of China, only 160 out of 3,187 missionaries have left on the account of the war."[59] The prevailing attitude was to remain in China, and as late as 1940, three years into the conflict, a writer for *The Intelligencer-Leader* quoted a retired admiral's praise of the courage exhibited by missionaries: "Our missionaries, doctors, and educators have, as a rule, remained at their posts and carried on their work in the face of great difficulties and real physical danger.... In every province the mission hospitals have won the affection of all communities."[60] The missionaries' fortitude and devotion would be further tested as the US entered the war.

1941 and Beyond

The end of 1941 brought about drastic changes to the lives of the RCA missionaries of the Amoy Mission. Following Japan's surprise attack on Pearl Harbor on December 7, America entered the conflict, declaring war on Japan the next day and thus ending the neutral status of the missionaries. Alma Vander Meer recalled that on the morning of December 8, they "woke up and saw the Japanese flag waving on our school flag pole, so the much-dreaded moment had come. America was involved in the war, and we were caught in Japanese territory."[61] David Angus, the then eight-year-old son of RCA missionaries William and Joyce Angus, remembered "looking down into our yard and seeing a Japanese soldier in full uniform standing guard with his rifle and fixed bayonet" on that day.[62] American and British nationals on Gulangyu were detained by the Japanese on mission-owned

---

59. Board of Foreign Missions, Reformed Church in America, *One Hundred and Sixth Annual Report of the Board of Foreign Missions*, 6.

60. Rear Admiral Harry E. Yarnell, former Commander-in-Chief of the Asiatic Fleet, quoted in "For China..."

61. Alma Vander Meer, interview, transcript, 30.

62. David Angus, sermon delivered at First Presbyterian Church, Lansing, Michigan, n.d.; shared by Angus with the author in May 2014.

property, where they were held until freed in exchanges of prisoners after negotiations between their respective governments and Japan. Before their work was halted due to the change in their political status, from 1937 to 1941 the missionaries provided tens of thousands of Chinese civilians with the necessities to survive in the face of a foreign invasion. Even after 1941, William Angus, who had escaped internment because he was in inland China at the time of the US declaration of war, remained in unoccupied China until the end of the war, carrying on as an evangelist in the face of malnutrition and malaria.[63]

The Gospel was embodied by the missionaries not only in their words, but also in their actions. Their unflagging devotion to God and commitment to the Chinese people anchored the Christian doctrine concretely in their world. By providing medical treatment, food, shelter, schooling, religious instruction, and encouragement, the RCA missionaries cared for the physical, educational, and spiritual needs of Chinese refugees in the first years of the Sino-Japanese War of 1937–45. The message of Jesus Christ in John 14:12 is that anyone who "believes in me will also do the works that I do; and greater works than these will he do, because I am going to the Father." The RCA missionaries in China manifested this message.

Epilogue

From the inception of the Amoy Mission in 1842, RCA missionaries sometimes faced both a hostile populace and an antagonistic government. Missionaries of all denominations were seen as agents of imperialist subversion of Chinese culture and were therefore often regarded with suspicion. The outbreak of the Second Sino-Japanese War helped to alter the prism through which the Chinese viewed missionaries and Christianity. Looking back upon this period of indescribable suffering some twenty years later, Searle Bates was able to pen these words: "The immense humanitarian services undertaken by the Christian organizations themselves, and their conspicuous or substantial roles in other social services, were rewarded by grateful appreciation which lessened old prejudices and fostered new understanding of Christian and missionary motives and character."[64]

---

63. David Angus, sermon delivered at First Presbyterian Church, Lansing, Michigan, n.d.; shared by Angus with the author in May 2014.

64. Bates, "The Protestant Enterprise in China, 1937–1949," 3.

During the war, even the Chinese Communist Party recognized the merit of the missionaries and worked briefly with those stationed in north China to bring aid to the Chinese people. The resolve of the missionaries to stay and provide relief to refugees during what is now referred to as the Asian Holocaust endeared them to numbers of Chinese who witnessed their work firsthand, as well as to others who heard about it. The missionaries were very aware that this was the hour of their witness, as can be seen in the 1940 article in *The Intelligencer-Leader* mentioned at the beginning of this chapter; it quotes a Chinese writer's tribute to the Christian men and women serving in China: "Today, after two years of hostilities, the Christian missions in China have built for themselves a record of which they may be justly proud. They have preached the gospel not with words but by a practical demonstration of the love of God and the brotherhood of man."[65] In their acts of sacrificial service, the missionaries showed themselves to be true believers in Christian doctrine and outstanding examples of humanitarianism.

Following World War II, however, with China torn by civil war between the Nationalists and the Communists, perceptions of missionaries changed again. With the Communists' triumph against Chiang Kai-shek and the Nationalists, the atheistic Chinese Communist Party was wary of foreign religious organizations operating in China. The Korean War further heightened anti-American sentiment, leading all missionaries to leave China by 1951. During the second half of the twentieth century, the charge of imperialism against missionaries became the dominant narrative. Not until the twenty-first century has there been a positive reconsideration of the work of missionaries in China and their contributions to Chinese society. The efforts of RCA missionaries during the Second Sino-Japanese War and World War II are now acknowledged in new scholarship. Historical narratives may change with political winds. However, there is no denying that an important legacy of the missionaries of the Amoy Mission is the survival of several tens of thousands of Chinese in southern China.

---

65. The article "For China . . ." quotes an "eminent Chinese writer" but does not give the writer's name.

Bibliography

Primary Sources

Angus, David. Interview. July 21, 2014.

———. Sermon. First Presbyterian Church, Lansing, MI.

Barnett, Robert W. "Isolated China." *Far Eastern Survey* 11/15 (July 27, 1942) 167–69.

Bates, M. Searle. "The Protestant Enterprise in China, 1937–1949." In *Frontiers of the Christian World Mission since 1938: Essays in Honor of Kenneth Scott Latourette*, edited by Wilbur C. Harr, 1–22. New York: Harper & Brothers, 1962.

Board of Foreign Missions, Reformed Church in America. *One Hundred and Sixth Annual Report of the Board of Foreign Missions of the Reformed Church in America*. New York: Reformed Church, 1938.

Clarence H. Holleman Papers. W95-1196. Joint Archives of Holland, Holland, MI.

Intelligencer-Leader (1938–1940). Clippings of the articles from *The Intelligencer-Leader* used in this chapter are kept in the collection Jeannette Veldman Papers. W89-1012. Joint Archives of Holland, Holland, MI.

Miner Searle Bates Papers. Record Group No. 10: Box 4 Folder 59. The Nanking Massacre Archival Project. Yale Divinity School Library. https://web.library.yale.edu/divinity/nanking/documents.

The Old China Hands Oral History Project (1976-1977). H88-0113. Joint Archives of Holland, Holland, MI.

Secondary Sources

De Jong, Gerald Francis. *The Reformed Church in China, 1842–1951*. Historical Series of the Reformed Church in America 22. Grand Rapids: Eerdmans, 1992.

Lu, Suping, ed. *A Mission under Duress: The Nanjing Massacre and Post-Massacre Social Conditions Documented by American Diplomats*. Lanham, MD: University Press of America, 2010.

MacKinnon, Stephen R., Diana Lary, and Ezra F. Vogel, eds. *China at War: Regions of China, 1937–1945*. Stanford: Stanford University Press, 2007.

Spence, Jonathan D. *The Search for Modern China*. 2nd edition. New York: Norton, 1999.

Varg, Paul A. *Missionaries, Chinese, and Diplomats*. Princeton: Princeton University Press, 1958.

White, Chris, ed. *Protestantism in Xiamen: Then and Now*. Global Diversities. Cham, Switzerland: Springer Nature, 2019.

"The New Map of China, Prepared for Missionaries and Travellers," 1937 revised edition, available through Kwang Hsueh Publishing House in Shanghai. In addition to railways and highways, it also shows mission stations. Folder "Maps, n.d.," William R. Angus Jr. Papers, H00-1381, Joint Archives of Holland.

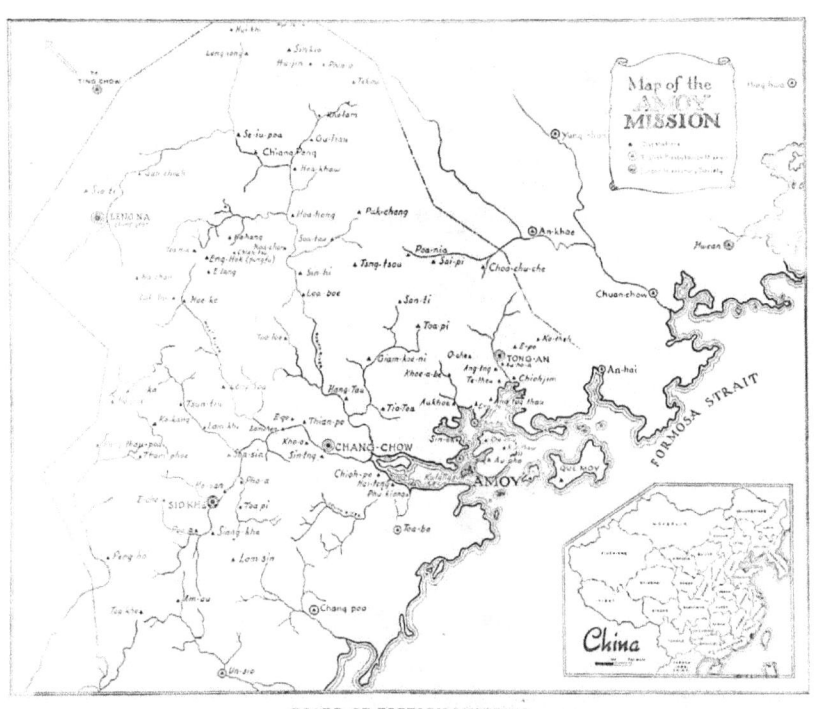

A map of the Amoy Mission published by the RCA. It shows mission stations of the RCA as well as those of the English Presbyterian Mission and the London Missionary Society. Members of the Amoy Mission had good relations with missionaries of these two British missions. Folder "Maps, n.d.," William R. Angus Jr. Papers, H00-1381, Joint Archives of Holland.

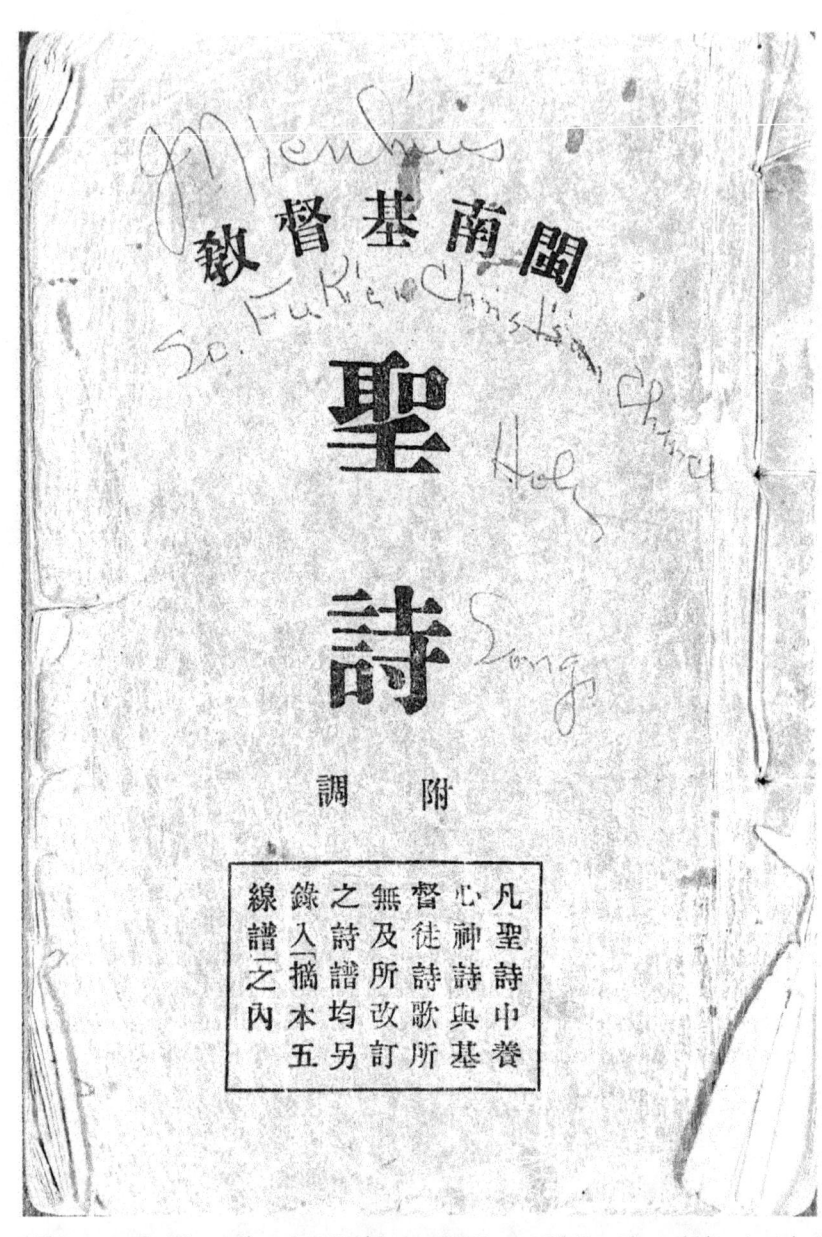

The cover of a Minnan (south Fujian) hymnal, *Minnan Jidujiao Shengshi* (in pinyin). Folder "Songbook (Chinese), 1934," Jean Nienhuis Papers, W96-1208, Joint Archives of Holland.

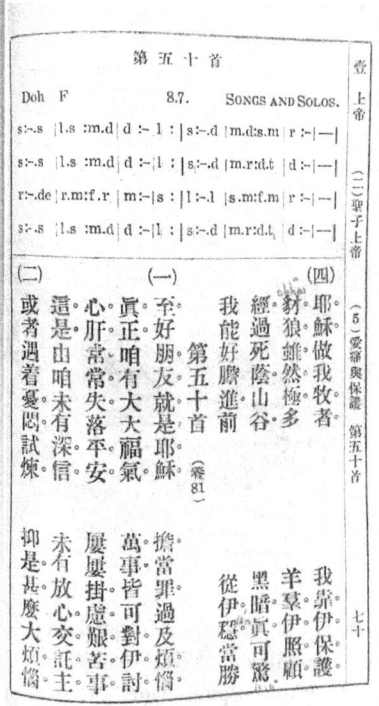

Hymn 50, "What a Friend We Have in Jesus," from the Minnan hymnal *Minnan Jidujiao Shengshi*. Folder "Songbook (Chinese), 1934," Jean Nienhuis Papers, W96-1208, Joint Archives of Holland.

Hope and Wilhelmina Hospital. Hope (the men's hospital) is on the right side of the picture; Wilhelmina (the women's hospital) is on the left. The one-story building in the center is the hospital chapel. The three-story building in the background is the Nurses' Home. Folder "Hope and Wilhelmina Hospital, Kulangsu, Amoy, China, 1934–51," Jean Nienhuis Papers, W96-1208, Joint Archives of Holland.

The restored Hope and Wilhelmina Hospital. It is now the location of Kulangsu Gallery of Foreign Artefacts from the Palace Museum Collection. Picture taken by the editor in 2018.

The entire body of Hope and Wilhelmina Hospital gathered for a farewell to Jeannette Veldman, then the director of the School of Nursing, who was leaving for furlough in America, 1936. Folder "Hope and Wilhelmina Hospital, Kulangsu, Amoy, China, 1934–51," Jean Nienhuis Papers, W96-1208, Joint Archives of Holland.

Hope and Wilhelmina Hospital School of Nursing, 1940; a farewell to one of their members who was leaving to go to Singapore. "Photographs—Chinese groups, 1925, 1948, n.d.," William R. Angus Jr. Papers, H00–1381, Joint Archives of Holland.

Hope and Wilhelmina Hospital School of Nursing gathered in a farewell to missionary nurses Jeannette Veldman and Anne De Young, 1950. Folder "Hope and Wilhelmina Hospital, Kulangsu, Amoy, China, 1934–51," Jean Nienhuis Papers, W96-1208, Joint Archives of Holland.

The class presidents and vice-presidents of the 1925 graduating class of the Girls' Middle School run by the Amoy Mission on Gulangyu, which was divided into a junior high section and a senior high section. Folder "Photographs—Chinese Groups, 1925, 1948, n.d.," William R. Angus Jr. Papers, H00–1381, Joint Archives of Holland.

Delegates of the South Fujian United Synod to the Fourth General Assembly of the Church of Christ in China, which took place in 1937 in the port city of Qingdao, Shandong province. Tena Holkeboer and Christina Wang were the only two women of the group. Folder "Photographs—Chinese Groups, 1925, 1948, n.d.," William R. Angus Jr. Papers, H00-1381, Joint Archives of Holland.

William and Joyce Angus celebrating Easter with a Chinese congregation. Folder "Photographs—William and Joyce Angus and Miss Go Teaching Choirs, Easter Services, n.d.," William R. Angus Jr. Papers, H00-1381, Joint Archives of Holland.

Christina Wang and Tena Holkeboer. The two women were close partners in ministry. Folder "Photographs—The Sin Family, 1926, 1938, 1939, 1947, n.d.," William R. Angus Jr. Papers, H00-1381, Joint Archives of Holland.

Jean Nienhuis and Gim-siu Sio. Folder "Photographs—The Sin Family, 1926, 1938, 1939, 1947, n.d.," William R. Angus Jr. Papers, H00-1381, Joint Archives of Holland.